H🗘pe

Tim Costello

Hope

hardie grant books

MELBOURNE · LONDON

Published in 2012 by Hardie Grant Books

Hardie Grant Books (Australia)
Ground Floor, Building 1
658 Church Street
Richmond, Victoria 3121
www.hardiegrant.com.au

Hardie Grant Books (UK)
Dudley House, North Suite
34–35 Southampton Street
London WC2E 7HF
www.hardiegrant.co.uk

Cataloguing-in-Publication data is available from the National
Library of Australia.
Hope
ISBN 978 1 74270 375 6

Cover and text design by LANZ+MARTIN
Typesetting by Kirby Jones
Printed in China by 1010 Printing International Limited

To my parents
Russell and Anne Costello,
and my children
Claire, Elliot and Martin

All are central to my experience of hope

Hope is what sits by a window and waits for one more dawn, despite the fact that there isn't an ounce of proof in tonight's black, black sky that it can possibly come.

Joan D. Chittister, *Scarred by Struggle, Transformed by Hope*

Contents

Acknowledgements

There are many people named in the anecdotes I have included in this book. People who have helped to make these stories what they are, and have worked beside or with me in all sorts of places. For their part in my life I am grateful.

But there are also many unnamed who have made these experiences possible. And to them I want to express my deep appreciation. They range from the loyal staff at World Vision Australia and colleagues in other organisations or spheres of life, that work towards making the world a better and more just place, to good friends and family who have nourished and grounded me.

Of course my most important acknowledgement is to Merridie, my wife. She has worked on the text of this book helping me shape what was 'a stream of consciousness'. Her eye for detail helped as we talked over the experiences I have had, as well as some that she has shared with me. Considering together the topic of hope has focussed our minds in the light of the stage of life we are in, and the challenges we continue to face in our journey together. Life's best gift to us has been a marriage of minds, hearts and core values.

My thanks too go to Pam Brewster as the patient publisher from Hardie Grant who kept believing in it – even when I had produced little.

Tim Costello

Living with stories

We had the experience but missed the meaning.
T.S. Eliot, *Four Quartets*

I grew up with stories. Some were fairytales where the like of Red Riding Hood was gobbled up by a big bad wolf. Others were of little children who would be put in ovens and cooked. Thoroughly gruesome, I know, but I now realise that, told in the presence of a trusted and loved adult, they were needed to mediate a worldview that even as a child I could absorb. Namely, that there is evil in the world and I will only be safe if I take it seriously. In this book, I will tell stories and personal anecdotes that give me hope to challenge evil and big problems.

Stories are the way we make sense of experience. I loved the ones about brave cowboys saving the day, and stories of resilient and courageous pioneers. Others were flights of imagination, read to me on the lap of my mother and grandmother, both of whom loved Dr Dolittle, Winnie the Pooh and Peter Pan.

But the stories that mostly captured me from a young age came from the Bible. They were told to me in reverent tones to emphasise their authority and sacredness. The Hebrew Scriptures are replete with champions like the boy David fighting the giant Goliath, leaders like Moses who stuttered and felt scared, and King Saul who battled his jealousy. I noticed, however, that it was the stories of the New Testament that were given the highest regard – stories told by or about Jesus. They were usually about everyday things that Jesus saw in the way of life around him. He used things that were hardly regarded as especially religious in his day: farming stories, housekeeping stories and family stories. They resonated with the lives he lived amongst. But they were open to be interpreted at deeper levels.

As an adult I still love stories. I recall very little of what I hear in a speech or a sermon, but a story – if told well – will stick with me, often for years to come. I generally find that on each trip I take, and often on each day of the trip, there will be something memorable that happens that illustrates my experience poignantly. Sometimes it will be in witnessing the struggle to survive that I will see and recognise something that I know is gold – something that needs to be shared beyond that moment and that place, that will inspire or challenge other people in other places because it inspired or challenged me.

I know that when I speak in public, which I do a lot in Australia, and am often asked to do in my travels, I can say hundreds of words and may even make some clever points, but it will be my stories that are most remembered. People love stories, so if, midway through a speech, I announce that I am reminded of a story, I see eyes light up – even eyes open up on occasions!

Perhaps it is the child within all of us – knowing that, with a story, we can take it as we are able. It is there for us to interpret or respond to as we can. It opens our imagination to possibilities.

In this book are anecdotes that come from where I have travelled with my work or impressions I have gathered as I reflect on my lived experience. I have used some of these stories over the years in various times and places. They have formed part of the tapestry of my life over the last twenty years. I see a few threads that run through the tapestry. A dominant thread is that of hope, for essentially I am a hopeful person who believes that life can and does have a way of giving us the impetus to keep going in hard times, and to keep working for what might otherwise seem like a 'hopeless' cause.

I am not a fatalist or one given to fanciful answers. I know that most of life is difficult and can be fraught with struggle. The symphony of anyone's life can have some loud and calamitous parts. It takes discernment, patience and deep listening to hear the soothing refrain of hope return.

If there is no hope, we as humans can become fatalistic with despair or cynicism. The Bible says that 'if there is no hope, the people perish'. So simple, yet so profoundly true.

The stories in this book illustrate my hope and come with the convictions I have gathered as I have reflected on my experience.

Take the next step

Young people often seek me out for advice about their careers. They usually start the conversation saying something flattering like they have followed me in the media or liked my stance on something. Some even say that one day they would love to be a CEO of an organisation like World Vision Australia and ask me to tell them how I got there. I find it a perplexing question to answer from an orthodox career-development point of view.

I was a suburban lawyer in Melbourne for two years. In 1980 I turned down an offer to enter a lucrative legal partnership to head off and study theology at a Baptist seminary for almost four years in Switzerland. Then, on returning home, I practised poverty law part-time and worked simultaneously as a Baptist pastor and preacher for a small inner-suburban church. After some years, I was caught up in some local issues related to housing for the poor in our area, so I was elected to the local council of St Kilda. A short time later I was elected as mayor, but my term was truncated a year later by the state government's decision to sack many local councils in order to amalgamate them.

At that point (in 1995) I returned to the Baptist

ministry, in the centre of the city of Melbourne, where I started a domestic charity with street people called Urban Seed. Along the way I was involved in plenty of public battles, trying to reform gambling and address homelessness and substance abuse. After working in that arena for ten years I became CEO of World Vision – Australia's largest charity. How is that kaleidoscope of a curriculum vitae linear, planned or capable of providing guidance to anyone?

So I sometimes tell anxious young people who are starting out on their own journey a story I heard when I was young. A father who was a coalminer took his son down the shaft into the underground pit where he worked. He said, 'Wait here in this lit space, as I need to go along this tunnel.' While the son was waiting for his father to come back, the light in the mine failed. He was in pitch darkness and screamed out for his father. Down the tunnel, he heard his father's voice command him to start walking towards him. The boy cried out that he could not see anything. His father said, 'Is the light on your helmet on?' The boy replied that yes it was, but it only threw light for one step ahead, and it was deep black beyond that. His father said, 'Well, take that step.' Of course, the boy did, and cried that he could not see any further. His father said, 'How much light can you see now?' The boy replied, 'Only about a step.' Back came the instruction, 'Well, take that step.' There was enough light just for one step at a time and, of course, by following the soothing advice, one step after the other, he finally reached the safety of his father's strong arms.

We would all prefer to see much further ahead. We want the road map and to know the short cuts. But usually we only have enough light for the next step. To get anywhere we must take that.

So to my young enquirers, I usually ask them if they are doing what they need to in this moment – maximising the light that is within them. Or are they trying to look too far ahead?

That story illustrates the way my life has worked, and I look back in genuine surprise at how far I have come. Take the step with the light you have. Walk in that light. It is sufficient.

God, you look white

I have been travelling internationally for many years now. This was so even before I took the job with World Vision Australia. Prior to that I went as an Australian Baptist speaker to places like Nagaland, India, Cuba and the Philippines. Sometimes it was to attend conferences, sometimes to go on fact-finding tours, and sometimes it was to speak at churches and meet local leaders. I love eating local food and staying in homes rather than hotels, so this often meant I was there amidst the squawking roosters rising before dawn, or sleeping on the floor along with my hosts.

Inevitably I picked up a few bugs. Some cleared quickly with a dose of Imodium. Others lingered and took me days to shake off.

Once my travelling with World Vision started in earnest, I found my body tested in ways unknown to that point. One memorable trip was to the Democratic Republic of the Congo. This is the country that had seen 'African's Great War' and four million people killed between the years 1998 and 2003 with the rest of the world hardly noticing. I had a week there with one of my most well-travelled staffers, who was doing some filming for our organisation. We were taken to some still dangerous settings and heard some desperate stories. Within two days I began to feel unwell. The symptoms got worse and Steve, who was filming me, paused with camera in hand and said, 'Tim I know these Congolese are dark but God, you look white.'

I was rushed to a bush church clinic. The nurse came at me with the biggest needle I had ever seen. I said, 'I don't care what I've got. Please do not stick that in me.' They did anyway, and soon told me it looked like I had malaria. I lay there thinking, 'Yeah but where else has that needle been?' but by then I was delirious and truly did not care. Whatever precautions I had taken had not worked. I knew I had never felt as bad. I don't remember much about the next few days. I went through heat, sweat, heart palpitations, more heat and weakness like I had never known.

My phone was not working. I had not spoken to my wife, Merridie, for five days. She had no idea of the state I was in and it was clearly only getting worse. In desperation, we decided to try to get home. I made it on a local flight to the Nairobi airport and remember lying on the floor in the passenger terminal.

Steve left me for a time as I drifted in and out of consciousness, hallucinating at times. I opened my eyes to see him walking towards me with a two-foot-tall carved crucifix! In my delirium I thought, 'So this is it. He knows something they have not told me.' Steve, bless him, a lapsed Catholic, had, in his anxiety, thought maybe he could get me something to help … and this wooden cross with carved black hands on it was what he found. Perhaps it was the closest thing he could find to a priest! To me, all it symbolised was his utter conviction that I was dying.

I was finally able to ring Merridie and weakly told her I probably had malaria and had never felt as bad. She told me to come straight out of there and assured me she would clear the decks for as long as I needed to recover at home. I had no flight booked yet from Dubai, but didn't tell her that! She tells me now that I told her I honestly was not sure I would make it, but I have no recollection of saying it.

Somewhere in the next six hours the medication kicked in. By the time I reached Dubai I was able to eat and sit and talk sanely. On the next leg, I even started to enjoy a laugh.

You can imagine Merridie's surprise when I bounced into the house a morning or two later. She had prepared all and sundry for my demise, or next to it. Yet here I was, ready to plunge back in.

And in my bag I carried the carved cross. It remains on the dining room wall in our home, and is a reminder that life has some noteworthy dark moments.

A bug that would not go

The cyclone in Myanmar in 2007 was intense for me on a number of counts. Some 130,000 people died with the ferocity of the winds and floods. I just knew that I had to get up there, as our 800 Burmese staff were shattered and demoralised. But getting in was not that easy. The regime refused visas and said that the situation was under control. In truth, the regime was paralysed and thousands died needlessly when they could have been reached with a co-ordinated relief effort.

I hassled the Department of Foreign Affairs and got the mobile number of the Burmese ambassador in Canberra, as there was no joy on getting visas from the embassy. He sounded very surprised when I rang him directly and said, 'Tim Costello! I have seen you on TV.' He initially refused me because, according to the party line, his government had it perfectly under control. But I continued to talk to him, refusing to hang up. He was polite and said, 'You know, I have seen you on television a lot.' After a bit more stalling, the breakthrough came: 'Yes, I will approve a visa.' Being a D-grade celebrity sometimes has advantages.

The awful dilemma I had upon arrival was how to get permission to get our supplies through the checkpoints. The military would order them handed over. We wanted to be sure that they were reaching the desperate people.

I met the general in charge of health and welfare. He sat high on a wooden throne with carved elephant heads on the arms. I entreated him for a letter to get our World Vision trucks through. After much pleading, he gave the barest nod of his head and our World Vision translating staff whispered, 'Quick, thank him and let's go.' I asked what had happened and they explained that he agreed, but we had to write the authorisation letter and get him to sign it immediately, before he changed his mind.

That letter was gold. Military barriers miraculously opened, and we could get aid to the affected areas. But now we faced an awful choice. Despite these few wins, the trickle of global humanitarian relief was still pitiful compared to what was needed – and so I took the risk and decided to do a global media campaign, knowing that we could get thrown out. I remember BBC and CNN journalists coming to interview me with their cameras hidden, because most of them were in there illegally or only on tourist visas. Some interviewed me with hats and false moustaches, knowing that as soon as their stories went to air they would be tracked down and thrown out. Unbelievably, I was not thrown out – and, after nearly a month of stonewalling by the regime, the global pressure from Ban Ki-moon and the international community saw the aid pipeline flow and the country start to open to a full relief effort.

After a week with our staff working under intense pressures to meet the demands, I was exhausted and ready to leave but found myself feeling sick. When I arrived home, nothing seemed to make medical sense. I was basically house-bound, losing 15 kilograms over the next two months. After being mucked around by some local doctors, a wonderful specialist said they would not rest until they found the cause. A rare bug was identified as the cause of my ailment and I was given medicine that killed it off. But, even more surprising, after the battery of tests it was suggested that I was gluten intolerant. Getting off gluten meant I suddenly had energy, and from that point on I have never felt better.

The only downside has been the discovery that what makes food taste good is called 'gluten'!

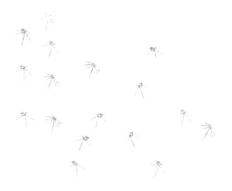

The gold standard

One of the most interesting parts of the world that I have visited is Nagaland in north-east India. A generation or two ago, this was an area where there were still pockets of headhunters. Skulls can still be seen dangling from the doorframes of some huts. Now the Nagas are Christians; indeed, due to a successful missionary endeavour in the early 1900s, they are mainly Baptists. For me, at least, that is preferable to headhunters.

There are over forty different tribes and villages situated among high mountains and perched on impossibly sheer slopes. The sense of tribe and place in Nagaland is so tremendously strong. Such security is provided by the knowledge of their ancestors and the inherited way of life. I have lived in seven different homes, in quite different places and socio-economic areas, and I have sensed that I have developed slightly different personas in each new context in order to cope. It makes me feel fragmented and poor in story compared to what I saw in Nagaland. They have a strong, unequivocal sense of connection to land and language, identity and embedded history, cultural dress and dance.

It is cold for much of the year, so full-length coats and shawls of beautiful colours drape their frames. In some of the areas, bright colours represent different roles. In one village, the teachers wore blue and the elders and lawgivers wore red. Fine hand-stitched work adorned these bright clothes.

One morning I was to address the village where I was staying at the 6 am prayer meeting. (Yes, the whole village rises each day to attend a prayer meeting!) I remember seeing the usual colours and spotting a person adorned with a gold coat. It was a knockout. I asked my host what that colour represented and was told that it indicated a person who has given a feast of merit. I looked quizzically at my host, who responded in surprise – surely my culture had feasts of merit? 'No,' I said, 'that's new to me.' So he went on to explain that in Naga culture, when you become rich – meaning you have a lot of pigs and bags of rice – you can choose to throw a feast of merit. This means hosting a party for the whole village, particularly the poor, which might go on for two weeks or a month – whatever time it takes to liquidate all your assets. When everything is gone, you have a glorious gold cloak placed on your shoulders in a ceremony of great respect. Then you start again with nothing – all except for your gold cloak. I recall telling him that I was pretty sure I had never heard of anything like a feast of merit in my culture.

It amazed me. Here was an avenue to recognise that we come to this world with nothing and certainly leave taking nothing with us, so the point of wealth is for now – to celebrate community, to bless others and to feed the poor. Relationships and care of others, not possessions or material superiority, are truly the gold standard.

We don't have feasts of merit in Western culture. But we have plenty who don gold who have never deserved it. In recent days maybe Bill and Melinda Gates are the closest we have to gold-coat bearers. Certainly the industrialist philanthropist Andrew Carnegie was right when he said the man who dies rich dies disgraced.

Overspeeding

When travelling in a different country, it is often a challenge to know what the customs are – especially when it comes to the money and tipping. We hear that a lot of corruption, or 'baksheesh', is because cops, members of the military, teachers and many others in the developing world are not paid enough in their salaries to keep their families alive.

I was driving with my Indian friend Eddie in New Delhi when the police pulled us over for 'overspeeding'. He said the fine was 1500 rupees. Eddie said it was 300 rupees. They settled somewhere in the middle.

As the cop left, he said, 'And your tyres are bald, so you are lucky it is not Tuesday as we do bald tyres on Tuesdays.' I asked Eddie how he knew how to negotiate the fine and he said, 'I looked at the insignia on his cap and uniform and worked out his seniority and what would be a fair amount given his rank.' So I realised that there was a sort of rational calculation! Just like tipping.

We in the West are very critical of this open form of corruption. But I got thinking about this after a New York cabbie screamed at me for forgetting to tip him. Embarrassed, I stumbled back and tipped him. What is it with tips? Are they really about rewarding excellent service, or are they our form of cultural corruption and a rational calculation? When a waitress or cabbie cannot live on their wage and feed their family without tips, do we not have a slightly more palatable mirror situation to the institutionalised corruption in developing nations?

Would it not be better to pay a fair wage and deal with good or bad service in a truly transparent way? So that if you tip it is because you really have appreciated someone's manner and service?

Of course, it takes honesty with oneself not to fall for the lure of a little extra. I remember a cabbie in Melbourne who recognised me and spent the trip telling me why he admired me. He saw me as one who stood for honesty and ethics and that, in his opinion, was exactly what we were losing in our nation. He pumped me up to a pretty high altitude and was eloquent with chapter and verse of the people and politicians he knew who were dishonest.

We got to the destination and he said it had been a pleasure to have that conversation – so different from the usual stuff he put up with every day. He turned to attend to the receipt. As he did so, without a moment's hesitation he said, 'Now I guess it is you reclaiming reimbursement from your employer, so how much do you want me to write on the receipt?'

'Well,' I replied, 'just the actual fare.'

Without blinking or looking at me again he said, 'Of course, mate, of course.'

Some things are easier to talk about in abstract than to actually follow through in practice!

God understands as
I am a poor man

I had arrived in Maputo, Mozambique, late one evening and checked into the VIP Hotel near the beach. Jet-lagged and unable to sleep, I wandered out at midnight for some fresh air and walked absent-mindedly about 50 metres down the street from the hotel.

Out of nowhere, two policemen with rifles slung over their shoulders crossed the street and asked for my documents. I stuttered that my passport was in my hotel room. They snapped that in Democratic Mozambique, the law required that documents must be carried on your person at all times. I apologised and explained that I had just arrived from Australia, and in Democratic Australia we did not have that law. I promised that I would not make this mistake again.

Not satisfied with my answer, they said they would have to arrest me and take me to the police station. I protested and asked one of them to accompany me to my room, only 50 metres away, where I would show them my documents. They refused and grabbed my arm and said if I did not come with them immediately, they would be ringing for a police car and back up. I asked what would happen to me at the police station and they explained I would be locked up for twenty-four hours and then fined on release. Again I protested that this was completely unacceptable. I had important meetings to attend in the morning. The one holding my arm then looked intently at me and asked me if there was another way we could solve this problem.

'Okay, how much do you want?' I said.

After some haggling we settled on $100, with me protesting that it was wrong and an example of the corruption that was totally against the values of World Vision, the organisation I work for. That had little or no effect! No sooner had I handed over $100 than the other policeman reached across and shook my hand and said, 'Thank you and the Lord will bless you.'

Staggered at what he said, I replied, 'I am not sure He will.' I asked him if he was a Christian.

He smiled and said, 'Yes, I am Pentecostal and my friend here is Catholic.'

'Well I am a Christian too,' I replied. 'Don't we Christians believe that God sees everything?' They both nodded. Then I went on – 'Well then, God has seen what just happened between us and thinks this is wrong.'

'No,' said the Pentecostal, 'God will bless you because you have helped us.'

I ignored that comment. 'The great thing with Christian faith is that when we do wrong we can repent and God totally forgives us,' I continued. 'Repentance would mean that you give me back my money.'

He shook his head and said, 'No, God understands because I am a poor man and he will bless you for helping us.' At that he turned and started to walk off. His Catholic friend obligingly went with him.

Feeling furious, compromised and theologically challenged, I walked back into the VIP Hotel, got my passport and walked out again, determined to show them this was all very wrong. Of course, they were gone. But down the street two other Mozambicans saw me stressing and approached me and asked me what was wrong. I explained how I had just been stung for $100 by a couple of 'Christian' cops. A man named Felipe introduced himself and said that made him so angry – 'This is an example of why we have problems in this nation!' He told me he was the nephew of the police commissioner. 'Come with me,' he pleaded, 'and we will help.'

I smiled, thinking, Oh no, now this could end up costing me a grand! I thanked them and declined.

He said, 'I am serious so if you won't come with me, just stand here and let me make a call.' After fifteen minutes and a few telephone calls, I thanked them for trying to help and told them I was going inside to bed. Tiredness had now overwhelmed all my emotions. Felipe held his hand out to me in a stop sign and said, 'No, just wait a bit longer – it is fixed.'

Sure enough, five minutes later the same two cops came slowly walking towards me. They had already changed the money into local currency but, with Felipe standing over them, they counted out a full $100 worth of shillings into my hand. I was astonished.

I thanked them all and reiterated to the policemen that what they had done was right. I told them I forgave them and that I was confident God forgave them too. They said nothing. So I asked them what they were going to do now. The Catholic said they were going home to bed. It had been a bad night!

So it had. Afterwards, on reflection, I knew it could have been a lot worse for me. I learnt a lot that night about self-care in new countries. But I also trust the Christian policemen learnt a bit too.

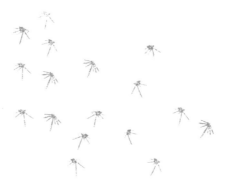

The arc that bends
towards justice

Martin Luther King said the arc of the moral universe is long, but it bends towards justice. Sometimes it bends very slowly. In February 2012, an old lady called Viola died in Melbourne at the age of 100. My brother-in-law, Harley, was taking the service, and he rang to tell me that Viola's sister was Alma Tirtschke, who had been found murdered in 1921 at the age of twelve in Gun Alley, Melbourne. It was a sensational story in the press at the time. An innocent young girl out on a short errand for her mother had been found brutally raped and strangled.

Hearing about Viola's death brought a few things to mind for me. I recalled opening a macabre exhibition of death masks at the Old Melbourne Gaol for the National Trust of Australia. It included death masks (like Ned Kelly's) and, in the cells situated near the gallows, letters and memorabilia from those who had been incarcerated in the cells were displayed.

Before my speech was to commence, I looked through the exhibition and paused to read some of the stories. That was where I read of Colin Campbell Ross. He was a wine merchant who worked close to Gun

Alley. Campbell Ross had been arrested when hairs resembling those of Alma Tirtschke were discovered on a blanket in his house. He was tried and hanged, all within nine months – such was the public outrage at this terrible crime.

I had never heard of Colin Campbell Ross, but was fascinated by his Bible: it was lying open to Psalm 26 and he had underlined a verse stating 'Oh Lord I am innocent'. In pencil, he had protested 'this is me' in the margin of the Bible. After his execution, his mother had pleaded for his remains – but she was denied them, and he was buried in the jail with others executed there. Viola Tirtschke and her parents suffered a terrible loss, but at least they had the comfort of knowing justice had been done to the man who had inflicted this horror upon young Alma.

My attention was caught by letters lying next to the Bible. The letters were from Reverend J. Goble, the Baptist minister in Footscray at the time – and the man I regard as the greatest Baptist minister in Australian history. Reverend Goble was almost alone in believing in Campbell Ross's innocence. He ministered to him up to the moment of death. I remember thinking if Reverend Goble defended him against a howling public lynch mob who demanded his death, there must be something to this claim.

That day at the exhibition I spoke with some researchers who were painstakingly researching Campbell Ross's file. A few years later, they had a breakthrough. The hair, purportedly Alma's, found on his blanket was still in the police files from 1921. DNA tests all these years later proved conclusively the hairs were not hers. An innocent man had been hanged. The state declared him innocent and issued the first posthumous apology in our state's history.

A short time later I stood under those gallows with the State Attorney General and some of Campbell Ross's family – they were in attendance to make a speech and receive a box containing his remains. His body had been exhumed and then cremated. The family wanted to honour the wishes of his late mother, who had always wanted a Christian burial for her son. That day his remains were buried with her in a country cemetery.

Also standing under the gallows that day with us were Viola's daughter and other members of the Tirtschke family. All those years later, they totally accepted that an innocent man had been executed. They were there in solidarity to right this wrong.

This time history indeed proved that the arc of the moral universe moves slowly, but it moves towards justice.

Caste and jackets

I have never been a member of the Melbourne Cricket Club (MCC) – it is a highly prized and annually pricey membership in our city that entitles its members to a seat and entry to the magnificent Melbourne Cricket Ground, our icon of sporting prowess. It is the stadium famous for the annual Boxing Day Test and the grand final of Australian Rules football at the end of each September.

It happened that one February I was invited as a guest of the president of the MCC to the Twenty20 Cricket game between Australia and the beleaguered Indian team (who ended up winning and redeeming some national pride). It meant arriving early for a dinner in the resplendent committee room. Outside the room, around 70,000 people were streaming into the stadium on that warm Friday night for the spectacle – a huge number of them decked in bright blue to support their Indian roots.

As it happened, before leaving home I had hurriedly changed into a shirt and tie and thrown on a light jacket that I often take when travelling overseas. It zips up at the front. In my mind it was not a night for anything heavier. Besides, my son Martin was coming, and one is lucky to see him out of jeans and a T-shirt – although I had told him to dress better. We met at the train station – him looking quite spiffy in a suit and tie (although loudly complaining about it, as only he can).

The dinner was silver service, held for some of the city of Melbourne's great and good. I immediately noticed that I was the only man not in a business suit. Seated at the president's table, it was hard to hide my zippered jacket. I fell into a conversation about how I had registered my children to become MCC members when they were very young. In my mind, this would enable them to join the Brahmin cast of 100,000 elite members in Melbourne's city of four million and separate them from the great unwashed untouchables. I knew it could be a twenty-year wait.

I explained to the president that I later lamented that in signing them up, but not myself, I had revealed a mental block in myself. I was born to a working-class father who never considered himself worthy of being an MCC member – and that meant I failed to put my own name down as well. I wanted better for my children, but subconsciously believed that was never to be my own destiny. Many years later I overcame this block and actually put my own name down, of course sponsored by an existing member (which is both a prerequisite and a filter, as you need to know one to get in). I am still waiting at fifty-seven to be invited in.

Curiously, the conversation with the president, who had played cricket for Australia in many countries, including India, turned to caste. He asked how it was possible that, in a democracy like India where some 400 million people are living on less than one dollar a day, we see appalling poverty tolerated alongside such extraordinary wealth and opulence. India has more millionaires than Australia has people. Yet it has almost as many absolutely poor as the whole continent of Africa – all in one nation. We talked of how the poor want better for their kids, but how caste thinking (the acceptance of one's fate at birth) still forms an effective mental prison. The fact that the caste system has been formally outlawed does not mean that caste thinking is not still prevalent.

At one point in the evening, I walked out towards another exclusive room in the MCC and was barred at the door. The attendant (who presumably would never be a MCC member himself) explained that a zippered jacket was unacceptable MCC dress and contravened the rules. I explained that I was guest of the president and that he had not mentioned this. The attendant smiled and said, 'Well, he would be too polite to tell you.' I felt immediate shame. I was still unworthy, just like my father. Then I started to shore up my personal defences. Was I not still the same person – with the same character – who had unknowingly contravened a protocol? So why such shame? Over a zippered jacket?

But these cultural nuances are powerful, and the prison they create is real. Poverty in our world is not just material. It is profoundly cultural and social. Until 1966, only a 'gentleman' could be captain of the English cricket team. Tradition and cricket go together and, as a passionate fan of the game, along with millions of impoverished Indians who constitute 'the wretched of the planet', it is a parable of caste and cultural challenge to the status quo.

A matter of judgement

MasterChef has been one of the most popular shows on Australian TV. I was asked to be a guest judge on the night that the Dalai Lama was the special guest. Do not ask me why the Dalai Lama chose to do this thing or why I did, other than to show respect to him. The test for the seven contestants in this episode was to cook something vegetarian for His Holiness. That in itself revealed the first surprise, as we discovered that the Dalai Lama is not a vegetarian. Yes, all of life is sacred and we should not kill and eat, but Tibetan Buddhists cannot get enough protein to survive, so as long as someone else kills the animal, they eat meals with meat.

Naturally the contestants were extremely shaky at cooking for such a world-famous figure, and each had to explain their choice of meal and intention. Most spoke of the Dalai Lama's simplicity and moral clarity, so they were cooking something simple and clear. One of the contestants, Ally, knew she'd had a terrible morning in the kitchen with her dumplings, and burst into tears, crying that she had let him down. Tears make gripping viewing in TV-land and, as the cameras zoomed in to catch her distress, His Holiness reached across the table and asked for her hands. Holding them tight in his own, he just calmly said, 'You know what? It really does not matter. It doesn't matter.'

Words of pure sanity in a moment of surreal televised 'real-life tension'. After a few of us had been invited to give a blessing for the meals, one by one the contestants brought them out and served us and stood watching our enjoyment. The chefs who anchor the show kept peppering His Holiness with the same question after each course – what did he like? They were not getting much help. He just liked it all. 'Well, what particularly?' He said he liked the bread and giggled. The bread! So the chefs took a more pointed and direct approach with His Holiness. 'Did you prefer this dish to the previous one?'

He said, 'No, just the same.'

'Well, was the next dish different and tastier?'

'No, it was good just like the last one.'

I could see the fear mounting that at this rate we would not have a program. Of course, we the other guests chipped in with our preferences, and in my case I offered a patter of confected culinary verbiage. My modus operandi was simple: as long as the vibe is right with the cooking zeitgeist, forget whether the words mean anything.

I turned to the Dalai Lama and said, 'Your Holiness, as a Buddhist you are not allowed to judge, are you?'

He smiled and said, 'No, we Buddhists must never judge. As monks we go from house to house with our empty bowls and whatever food is put in it we are thankful. No, we do not judge. We will never judge because that would be wrong.'

The lights suddenly switched on in the minds of the compere judges. So they were asking him, for the sake of dramatic tension for their TV program, to help pitch a real contest and do something that contradicted the very essence of his faith. I'm sure they wondered who had done the program research on that one. One of the judges immediately turned to me and asked my view on the contestants and their two courses and I said, 'Well, I am more than happy to judge. I am a Christian.' It got a laugh, but seriously they appreciated my capacity to help carry the day.

Of course, Jesus also said, 'Judge not that you be not judged.' But he believed, as do I, that ultimately there would be a final wrap up – a judgement day when the curtain falls rather than endless cycles of reincarnation. And what will happen there? Well, if you read The Gospel of Matthew 25, it is bit like having the exam questions in advance. It tells us the basis for this judgement, so there are no surprises. The nations are gathered before the throne of God and they are divided into sheep and goats – heaven and hell – on the basis of a couple of simple questions. When I was hungry did you feed me? When I was thirsty did you give me something to drink? When I was naked did you clothe me? When I was in prison did you visit me? When you did all this to the least of my children you did it to me. And by contrast when you failed to do this you failed me.

To speak of judgement makes a lot of tolerant people nervous today. It sounds harsh and arrogant. But I need to believe in judgement. Too many innocent people have suffered and too much evil has been done by others, without any accountability or consequence. Judgement is important for my sense of wellbeing. It is a relief to believe in it.

No judgement at all is a far worse fear for me.

Bono the bard

I was addressing a Make Poverty History concert in late 2006 and had a large crowd of young people in front of me in the mosh pit. The concert was being held in Melbourne the night before the G20 finance ministers were set to meet in the city. It also coincided with Pearl Jam and U2 being in town to do huge concerts over the following few days. Eddie Vedder and Bono, who had been told of our concert, made brief surprise appearances and sang some duets to the shock and delight of the crowd. They were keen to support the cause and to further call for an increase in foreign aid to address the Millennium Development Goal of alleviating poverty.

After the concert, a few of us went out to dinner. I realised that if Bono was not known as one of the world's greatest singer/songwriters, he would have been famous as one of the world's best storytellers. An Irish bard, indeed. So good was he that Eddie hardly said a word and just kept writing notes on the paper tablecloth in front of him. After three hours of listening to the flow of talking and storytelling, Eddie meticulously folded his voluminous jottings into a neat square and quietly told us that for him it had been one of the best nights in memory.

Being the co-chair of Make Poverty History in Australia, I was fascinated to observe Bono's ability to work both sides of the political divide, both in our nation and beyond. He spent time with our prime minister and with our opposition leader. In the US, his relationships were not just with Democrats – he has built relationships with Republican congressmen who would not normally support increases in foreign aid for the world's poor. Their support gave President George W. Bush political cover to announce some of the most generous and remarkable aid initiatives in recent American history. I have seen evidence that support for initiatives to decrease the impact of AIDs and increase access to clean water does save lives.

Bono has copped a lot of criticism and has been dismissed as a hopeless romantic by some. The tone from economic hardheads is, of course he would believe in that fairytale of making poverty history, but remember: he is Irish – and an Irish rocker – and essentially, he is a poet, so why would you take him seriously?

Some twenty-five years ago, 60,000 children under the age of five were dying from malnutrition and preventable disease each day. Just two years ago, we had halved this number and seen it drop to 30,000 a day. Two years on, it is 21,000 a day. That number in a world of plenty is still obscene. But to those who say Bono or any of us in the Make Poverty History movements are adolescents and idealists: just take in these figures, and the enormous achievements they represent. These are lives. These figures represent children who now have access to clean water and to food. This is real hope. Remember also that for most of the world's rich governments, beating poverty has never been an urgent priority. In this regard, George W. Bush was an exception. For me, that is the best testimony to his presidency.

Bono's relationship with Republican congressmen and senators is interesting for another reason. Republicans act as custodians of the evangelical vote in the US, a vote that sees opposition to abortion and gay marriage as the critical issues, but Bono gently reminded them that the Scriptures say much more about the poor than either of these issues. This came to a head when many evangelical voters were outraged that President Bush had invited Bono to deliver the address at the 2006 Presidential Prayer breakfast – a high religious moment in life on Capitol Hill in Washington DC. Many Republicans were outraged at their own president and questioned whether Bono was even a Christian. Some refused to attend. But one congressman who did so, reluctantly and angrily, was later reported as saying, 'I went into that breakfast sure that Bono was not a Christian. After listening to him, I came out wondering if I was a Christian.'

This is part of what he said and is why I regard him as such a brilliant communicator in any forum – private (over dinner) or public. He mocked himself, given the controversy, and said:

If you're wondering what I'm doing here, here, at a prayer breakfast, well, so am I. I'm certainly not a man of the cloth, unless that cloth is leather … Look,

whatever thoughts you have about God, who He is or if
He exists, most will agree that if there is a God, He has
a special place for the poor ... Check Judaism. Check
Islam. Check pretty much anyone.

Bono remains a prophet for many of us toiling in this work. I admire how he has stayed with the issue of global poverty, unlike many celebrity UN Goodwill Ambassadors who start out with a blaze of publicity, but seem to quietly disappear and move on to the next assignment when their agents feel they need to tweak their image.

I had a moving exchange when I met with an Australian nurse named Sue Germein when I was speaking in Adelaide a few years ago. She told me she had been working in Ethiopia with World Vision in the terrible famine of 1984–6 and remembers Bono and his wife coming out before Live Aid in order to better understand the issue. She met them and showed them around, even though at that time she'd had no idea who he was. It was an exchange that transformed him into a passionate advocate. He spoke to me later of how her humble love and determination in that terrible crisis had inspired him. He went from there prepared for Live Aid and, of course, it went on to become a global first and a triumph.

An act of God?

O n Boxing Day 2004, a cataclysmic earthquake under the Indian Ocean caused a catastrophic tsunami to inundate the coasts of seven countries in the region. I had been CEO of World Vision Australia for only ten months at that time, but as soon as the story hit the news I knew I had no choice but to respond. The first reports came from Sri Lanka, where World Vision has a significant number of staff and projects. So in response to the staff's appeals, I jumped on the first plane available and went there.

On the road south from the capital, Colombo, on the way to the town of Galle, we drove past what was left of the Queen of the Sea passenger train. The train had been crowded, as any traveller on the subcontinent would expect, with around 1500 people packed into the cars returning to Galle for holy Poya (full moon) day.

Exact numbers are hard to come by but, after two immense walls of water first ripped the train from the tracks then hurled it like a toy another 100 metres inland, there were only around 200 survivors found alive.

I arrived in Galle, home to a once-thriving tourist industry and a famed, but now destroyed, cricket ground. The ground where Shane Warne had taken his 500th wicket was now surrounded by those suffering hunger, whose homes were destroyed, who had lost loved ones, who had barely escaped the waves and were suffering from a variety of injuries. I also saw the piles of bodies growing as more dead were found – many seemed to be just children. No-one prepares you for the smell of death. The stench coming from the piles was something I had never encountered before, and hope never to encounter again.

The Sri Lankans I met there stood looking out to the sea; before the tragedy it, along with tourism, made up 80 per cent of the town's economy. Those that could find words asked me, 'Why did this happen?' Others just stared out to sea blankly, hoping their loved ones swept away might return.

Anyone who has conducted a funeral or counselled those who suffer knows that profound grief and trauma are complicated states that are not remedied with even the best insights from faith or psychological traditions. Actions inevitably speak louder than words.

Touching and embracing even in a different culture is universal and stronger than words. While I was with these suffering Sri Lankans, if I could offer one small hope, it was that both believers and non-believers from around the world would not forget them or abandon them. And that this was where they could find a sign of God's presence, in the form of the compassion and action by the world's citizens and governments.

As I travelled back to Australia, I thought of the Church's history of grappling with the problem of suffering, the problem of evil. It divided theological responses to human evil from response to natural evil, or natural disasters.

Then a curious line from the film *The Silence of the Lambs* came back to me. Hannibal Lector asks Agent Starling: 'Look at me, Officer Starling. Can you stand to say I am evil?'

She replies, 'I think you've been destructive. For me it's the same thing.'

'Evil's just destructive? Then storms are evil, if it's that simple. And then we have fire, and then there's hail. Underwriters lump it all under "acts of God". But it is evil in its destructiveness.'

The clever dialogue between Starling and Lector, created by Thomas Harris (the novelist) and Ted Tally (the scriptwriter), illustrates two points. First, that evil is a problem not only for the church, but one that psychiatrists, sociologists, geneticists and criminologists have yet to fathom; and, secondly, this exchange reveals that we have long ago given up on the idea of God as the direct author of rain, hail and storms. Though ancient traditions saw rain as a sign of God's blessing, Jesus made plain that the rain falls on the honest and dishonest alike — so too, one could add, do hurricanes and tsunamis.

We live on a globe with a fragile ecological and geological balance. A few degrees change in the global temperature, and millions will perish. The tsunami was a very natural disaster, not an act of God punishing the world for its materialism, violence and selfishness, not a judgement on the sex trade in Thailand or the civil strife in Sri Lanka or the military rebels in Aceh, Indonesia.

With all its terrible and catastrophic consequences, the tsunami was predictable and is explainable. Continental plates grind against each other, producing earthquakes and sometimes tidal waves. It is a disaster that has a history, and such disasters will happen again.

In fact, if there were some direct relationship between morality and natural disasters, as was once thought, it would make God out to be an unconscionable bully to the coastal poor and a chief benefactor of cities such as Zurich, Palm Springs and Paris. And it would also make a mockery of Jesus's teachings about the special place for the poor in the heart of God.

God's power is not like our desire to move and shake the world. In each situation, it seeks to save what is lost, liberate what is in chains, heal what is broken and lift up those who have become tired. God is a carrier of burdens. And it is a privilege that we have the opportunity to work in solidarity, compassion and restoration with those whose burden is greatest. Consequently, I believe that acts of God are not the disasters themselves but rather the people who reach out in compassion and generosity to the victims of such tragedies.

Like everything in life, the tsunami of 2004 calls for a response and interpretation. Too often natural disasters more deeply affect the poorest of the globe: those whose dwellings are the least stable; those whose access to clean water, sanitation and medicines are the most tenuous; those with the least ability to receive disaster warnings and act accordingly.

And much of the suffering following natural disasters is exacerbated by poor planning, inequality and bad economics. In some of the South-East Asian countries affected by the tsunami, coral reefs have severely deteriorated and many have had up to half their mangroves destroyed. While the deterioration and destruction are the by-products of greater tourism and prawn-fishing opportunities, the downside has been a greater vulnerability to tsunamis and a contribution to the horrific loss of life.

Similarly, while cheap energy has produced greater economic growth, global warming and the resultant catastrophic weather changes could roll back all of these benefits in a generation. And the tsunami we witnessed may become the first of many great natural disasters of the twenty-first century.

Some of these are factors in our power to change, not responsibilities we can pass on to God. The immense aid effort and generosity from all over the world following the 2004 tsunami revealed the best of the human spirit. The phenomenal response reminds us that human solidarity and compassion for all people is the essence of human life *and* survival.

So if God is all-powerful, why did this happen on 26 December 2004? I'm wary of anyone who would profess an answer to this unanswerable question. But I will suggest that God was very active in the hearts and minds of millions around the globe after this event. The pain and trauma of those in the hundreds of places like Galle will continue for many, many years to come. But they will now find partners in that pain. And, hopefully, those burdens that can be shared will be.

In the West our context gives us the luxury of posing the question, 'Why did God allow this?' I have in more recent years visited all the countries affected by that tsunami. What I have noticed out in the places of greatest impact has been the hopefulness and tenacity of people to rebuild from scratch. And, interestingly, more often than not, their question is not 'Where was God on that day?' It is 'How could anyone live through such a tragedy without faith? How could I find the strength to start again and rebuild without my faith?' Context determines the question. Yes, faith might be all that they had, but it was the resource needed to get up again and restart, to create meaning and hope out of the chaos.

Hope shattered

I remember a time in my youth when the idea of having doubt was a bit of a worry. I was a leader of young people in a Baptist church as well as being a leader at the Christian Union at my university in Melbourne. So I was surrounded by peers who were for the most part committed Christians. My life was busy with prayer meetings, bible studies, lunchtime lectures and evangelistic coffee shops. It was a non-stop faith-building enterprise.

Or so I thought at the time. The truest bit was the 'non-stop' descriptor. There was no room for 'down' time, as we like to call it now. In all truthfulness, I hardly had time to pray – even though I exhorted others to develop their prayer life. My focus was all about leading the enterprise, keeping up the charge so others would find their place and join the momentum. No doubt I would have been good value in the trenches in the First World War!

So the idea of doubt had little room in my head, and no place in my language. It was like talking about sex or death in polite circles. One just did not go there.

But life has a way of catching up with us. Doubt came at me through a few experiences I had no time to duck.

The first was through a young man called Andrew who joined the Bible study group I ran on a Tuesday night. Andrew was bright and asked thoughtful questions. He had lived a bit, and looked like more of a hippie than your regular churchgoer. He moved in with some of the other guys in our group and proved to be an excellent cook.

I liked Andrew, as he would make strong eye contact and would come week by week with written thoughts from things he'd read in the Bible or in books I lent him. I gave my tried-and-true answers but sometimes felt they were a bit thin. He would look at me quizzically as if to say, 'Is that all there is?'

Andrew would always appreciate personal time with me. He told me he was having trouble sleeping and that his thoughts were swirling. I prayed with him. I even encouraged him to see a doctor. It was then he told me he had been in a psychiatric hospital in the months before he came to the church. I began to see a few signs that worried me.

He didn't give us time to take it further. Two days later, his housemate found him in their garage – shot through the head. No note left.

I led the large group of young people in our church through the shock and sadness – the empty feeling of helplessness when such a tragedy befalls a community. But in my own heart I felt the beginnings of a deep chasm. My words sounded hollow. I could not pray. My own sleep was disturbed.

Doubt comes in various shapes and sizes. For me at that time it came in the form of self-doubt and questioning the very essence of all that lay behind my strongly held beliefs. I had been trained and versed in formulas, but did they ring true? Did that hold water in real life?

It started me on a search that ended up taking me to a theological college overseas. I encountered a heap of more doubt along the way, but also discovered a way to think about and understand faith that was in harmony with my burgeoning passion for justice and human rights. It meant for me seeing God in the person of Christ as one who suffers with us.

A second experience was more recent. It was 2006 and I was in Darfur, Sudan, on my way home from some World Vision International meetings. I had been delegated to represent and report to the organisation on the progress of our work there. A staff member met me at the airport and I was taken by road to the far west where the camp was situated. This camp was set in a windswept landscape full of scrubby foliage. The tents that housed thousands of refugees seemed flimsy and vulnerable. The setting felt to me like something at the edge of the world. How could people exist here for weeks, months and even now for years?

On the first morning I was introduced to a woman who sat cradling an emaciated child. Through the translator, her story unfolded. Like many others, she had been raped in her village before fleeing the rampaging militia. She had four children, but one was ill – gravely so. Her choice was to either flee her ransacked home with the other three or face certain death by staying by her ill child. Again, it was the eye contact that got to me. Direct from her soul to mine. This was her choice, and she made it – only to face the death of yet another child on the pitiless trek to relative safety in this desolate wind-blown camp.

My words to her seemed clumsy. Despite crouching beside her, I felt large and overbearing. What was I doing there? Who did I think I was? What did I possibly know about such suffering and loss? Where was God in this mayhem?

After seeing the food and aid distribution sites, visiting with the staff there and hearing their reports, I got back onto a plane home a few days later. It was too easy to depart. Too easy to sit back and be waited upon; too easy to leave behind all I had witnessed and heard.

But her eyes remained with me and the story they told of such incomparable loss. Doubt was my companion on that trip home and beyond. Was the aid effective? Was there any way to bring changes within corrupt regimes and evil structures? Does good win over evil?

Such questions have informed much of my musing, praying and reading since that time. Doubt and questioning has enabled me to stay in the job – even as I have found hope in the midst of what seemed to be hopeless situations.

Doubt is not the opposite of faith; it is its Siamese twin. In my journey, the psalms of the Hebrew Scriptures have been the most helpful way of holding the two together. In the psalms I see a struggle by people of faith, both praising God for being in control and in the next breath screaming out in anguish, feeling abandoned and in despair.

My faith is now less replete with answers that seem conceptually watertight and more about living in a relationship with God. It is the daily rhythm of fully engaging the present between the bookends of having faith and experiencing doubt.

There's violence in me

Sometimes a TV interview can influence your life. That happened to me when I watched the last interview of Timothy McVeigh, the bomber of the Oklahoma FBI building, before he was executed in 2001. As I remember it, he was asked why he committed such a terribly violent act. He answered simply, 'Because my government is my teacher.'

The interviewer looked incredulous, responding, 'But you are an ex-marine and trained in weapons and their use. How could you do this?' Again, McVeigh repeated with cold anger that he had learnt everything from the American government; it was the model for his life. The interviewer, who assumed the American government was good and certainly not murderous, found this response utterly incomprehensible. He was just floored and perplexed. I wasn't.

This is sometimes called the shadow. The military is much honoured in the US, but internationally it also casts a dark shadow stretching from the My Lai Massacre in Vietnam to Abu Ghraib in Iraq.

Much has been written about the Germans in the 1930s. They were the best educated and most cultured of all the world's nations at the time. They led the world in music, maths, engineering and invention, and it shocked the world such a culture had perpetrated something as monstrous as the Holocaust. The shadow was always there but, left unaddressed, it wrought genocide. Australians still find it hard to accept the Stolen Children chapter in our dealings with our own Indigenous people. The then–prime minister Kevin Rudd's national apology was addressing this shadow, ending the stubborn refusal to admit to the damage the European settlers did.

Timothy McVeigh's awful crime led me to wonder if anger and violence are just embodied in bad cultures and in bad people. Can we rid the world of evil by going to war with or executing the bad apples? It took me some reflection to admit that all cultures and individuals need to face the inconvenient truth that there is violence and hatred within all of us – even if mercifully few are Timothy McVeighs. It was even a longer journey for me to face up to my part in that and name my own shadow.

The first feature piece written on me was a 1993 article in a major newspaper, *The Sunday Age*, entitled 'Saint Tim'. The title was a clever play on my title as a reverend and head of a street ministry in St Kilda. Even though I was chuffed at the time with having my story in print, looking back, it did not help my personal growth. I then had to live up to this title with its connotations of do-gooding and selflessness. Instead of being self-emptying (which is true of real saints), I knew I was sometimes self-promoting. If attacked, I knew I could go into self-defence mode, inwardly raging. I had a reputation to protect. Rather than refrain from revenge, whatever the provocation – as saints do – I could try to settle the score. I knew I was no saint.

The stronger the public light shines upon a person, the more intense the shadow. Perversely, to be regarded as 'good' leads to over-compensating – because the shadow self wants out. It wants to be known and recognised as part of the equation. It is the enemy within and, if denied, it only trips you up and makes you aggressive or depressed. But if it is the enemy within, it has to be embraced with self-knowledge and self-acceptance. Remember, it was Jesus who said, 'Love your enemies.'

But how? It is only possible if the light shining on this part of your nature is impartial and accepting. Any sniff of judgement makes the shadow side hide. That is why God's grace is so important for me. It is a truthful light that sees you for who you are, sees the worst and still loves, forgives and accepts. For me, it is part of a spiritual journey of discovering why I need certain things and finding the courage and discipline I need to unwind the rage and potential violence in me.

This journey that started with watching Timothy McVeigh led me later to musing on Abraham Lincoln. Lincoln's advisors were chiding him at one point, telling him that, since he had the political upper hand over his enemies, he needed to go in for the kill. Lincoln answered them by saying, 'But if I make my enemy my friend, do I not destroy my enemy?' In my view, Lincoln had faced up to his rage and shadow, and found a way to turn opposition and conflict into good.

So why not change the horizon?

In the terrible Gujarat earthquake in India in 2001, World Vision was doing its daily relief distribution of food. Thousands of people had lost their homes and food supplies, so there were long queues and line-ups. The caste context was so entrenched that it seemed unthinkable to do mass food distributions without agreeing to separate the lower castes from Brahmin with different food lines in different places.

But then the staff had a horizon-busting realisation. What better time could there be to remind them that the caste system, which had been outlawed in principle by the government, was over? Caste should make no difference, when they are all humans in need. It was a scary moment when they decided that there would be only one point of distribution – and no caste concessions. Would there be riots? They drew a deep breath and began.

It worked – the millennia of social scripting, which taught that some were superior and others inferior, ceased to make a difference that day. All lined up and collected together peacefully.

Only when the trappings are stripped back do we realise that we are all just fragile humans trying to get by, no matter what our birth rights.

In an Indian village in Chennai I met a twelve-year-old girl called Divya. World Vision had a project that had recently brought electricity to the village. Divya told me that before the electricity had come, each day her main aim had been to get though the day without being molested by men and to forage for whatever food she could find for the family. I asked her what her dreams were. She dreamed of staying in school and getting a university degree. But her father was poor, and struggled to give her anything. I asked her if the electricity had changed anything for her family. She said they used to sit in darkness, 'But now we have light.' Her father now had a bicycle repair stall and they had some more money. She was able to go to school. Her horizon, that had been limited to surviving each day unmolested, had moved to a horizon of hope for a future, and maybe even going to university.

Sometimes the horizon has to be chased. Our Citizens' Voice in Action program in Uganda taught a community that their government had a duty to provide health workers to them, under the national health policy. After organising and helping them lobby the government, some health workers were appointed. Everyone in the community celebrated their big win and the collective voice that had brought it about. They had won this, and were not just depending on an aid agency like World Vision to provide for them.

But soon, they noticed that the health workers were very patchy in their attendance. The reason was that they expected better housing accommodation. The community lobbied again and got housing built for them – and celebrated another win with their citizens' voice and political muscle. But after the housing was built, the health workers were still not attending. Again they asked why, and found out that there was no electricity in the housing – the workers would not attend and stay until there was. Again they organised and forced the local government to put the power on. Finally, they had health workers – and a dramatic turnaround began in health outcomes for the community. The horizon of better health for their children kept moving, but they themselves kept chasing it.

We must do something to help these poor people

My work, especially the visiting of poor communities or dealing with the after-effects of terrible disasters, often elicits a response from people I meet when back at home: they really admire what I do, as it must be so terrible to see those things. They are glad it is me doing it, as they themselves could never do that work. If I had a dollar for every time I have heard that, I would be a rich man!

All of us have psychological limits, and I do understand where people are coming from when they tell me this. I know acutely the feeling of helplessness that overcomes me when I leave a poverty-stricken area – especially when those eyes full of desperation follow me. If as a parent you cannot provide enough food or clean water for your child, you feel a terrible failure. Given that every generation tries to hand over a better life to their children, if parents cannot get them into school or have to withdraw them from school to work collecting sellable rubbish because of family poverty, the sense of failure can be overwhelming.

But there is a paradox. Development is not simply saying that we have the answer called wealth and they have a problem called poverty, so if we give them a bit of our wealth – in the form of aid – then we have done development. We have a problem, too. In our communities of affluence, there are fragmenting communities along with an epidemic of depression, youth suicide and drug abuse. In poor communities, I will often witness the opposite. I become invigorated as I see connections to extended family and real community. I hear song and dance and respect for land and tribe. I see children kicking a Coke bottle and having as much joy as our kids with all their gadgets. It often surprises me to think there is more joy with the poor than in our societies, where we have solved the economic challenge of supply.

The paradox is that our society also needs development – albeit of a different kind – and we can learn from these communities in a relationship of partnership. It is not just one way, nor just charity. I will never forget, years ago an aid organisation made a video called 'Unequal Worlds', comparing my home in Melbourne to a slum in Delhi. In the latter there was no running water in oppressive heat, and the home was set in a crowded slum. There was no comparison to my fairly standard four-bedroom house, with water on tap in three rooms. I knew what I would choose. But gnawing away at me was the misgiving that we had not told the whole story. In the slum it was evident there was community – people peeping round doorways, children laughing in the alleys. Our home was orderly (that day!) and quiet, our neighbours all inside their own sanctuaries. It was a disquieting comparison for a number of reasons.

These misgivings were inflamed when I saw a program on television where some Delhi slum-dwellers were taken to London for two weeks. There, a tour of typical city life was planned for them. They met people in their homes, local councils, sporting and community groups. It was fascinating to watch them get interviewed at the end of the trip and asked what they thought. Their consensus was that they must do something to help those poor people. They were so lonely and so bereft of community. Their old people were not cared for by the family, but shunted off somewhere where they waited to die. This was so sad. What could they do to help them?

Our parents and grandparents remember times when we did not trade community so lightly for convenience and affluence. I remember times with board games, singing around the piano and neighbours talking over the back fence. I have often wondered aloud with my mother (a counsellor) if the rapid growth in counselling services is directly proportional to the loss of community. Do we pay counsellors to listen in depth because we do not have friends who really know us and have that sort of time on their hands?

My 93-year-old father has often reminded me of those simpler times. He tells me that when he married my mother in 1953, they could not afford a double bed and slept on a mattress on the floor for the next two years. They got a car when they had saved enough to pay it off. I was ten years old by then. And a TV did not come till the next year. I get the point.

When we married in 1979, of course, we had a double bed, a car and a TV and, if starting out today, I am sure we would add a microwave, washing machine, clothes dryer, DVD player, laptop, and an iPhone as absolute necessities. Were our parents less happy? From my observation, they had a very strong sense of community and locality, as they would walk or bike to the shops and stop in the street and chat. My father would always travel to work in a car with other teachers. Their friendships were many and they were deep. My parents, in the same locality sixty years later, still tell us the news – who is doing well and who is battling and, sadly, these days more and more frequently, who has died. I admire how much they discuss caring for others and how well tuned-in they remain.

Is there a trade-off where community diminishes with growing speed and affluence? Poverty can be a poverty of relationships rather than things. Material achievement is a tricky benchmark for wellbeing. Naturally it is always relative, as we rarely compare ourselves to those with less. The energy and envy is always directed towards those with more.

My three children have reminded me over the years that longing for the old, simpler days is a disease of every generation as it gets older. They tell me not to get nostalgic and judge them, as they just do it differently – via Facebook and Twitter. They have a point about virtual communities, but only time will tell if they have more lasting friendships thanks to social media.

So the question I often ask myself is: who are the poor in this world?

Education as a
contraceptive

We now know that for every dollar earned by a woman, some 90 cents will flow to the family and kids, whereas only 40 cents for every dollar a man earns will go to the family. Men are still more likely to drink, gamble or otherwise blow the money. This is why microfinance loans are largely directed to women – and that disturbs not just the power of men, but also the power of moneylenders. They are used to threats of kneecapping to maintain their lucrative business and see our efforts as provocative. But to beat poverty, you must take risks – and the best, but riskiest, thing is to empower women. And the risk is worth it. For every year a girl stays in school, she will have 1.2 fewer children. Many say people are poor because they have too many babies. The implication is, if they stop having kids, things will get better. In fact it is the opposite. Beat poverty and give education and they will stop having kids. It is a rational choice for the poor, with few prospects and no social security, to have a number of kids who can care for them in bad health or old age. Our grandparents made the same choices of large families when we were poorer here. Every nation that has been lifted out of poverty has moved to zero population growth.

It is funny to think of education as a contraceptive. But a woman with an education will have the skills to run a business and just maybe the strength to resist the cultural pressure to marry a guy twenty years older who has two wives already. With an education and skills in numeracy, she can take a loan and open a roadside stall, or buy a sewing machine and make some of her own choices – maybe even the choice to avoid becoming a baby factory which, previously, was entirely up to men to decide. The tears I have witnessed when a woman gets her first loan of maybe $50 are gut-wrenching. Sometimes there are tears because it is the first time that woman had ever physically handled money. Only men had previously been allowed to touch it.

It will take generations to change this inequality. Change will require educating mothers and other women, not just men. In East Timor and Papua New Guinea, women die in childbirth needlessly. Simple treatable conditions of pregnancy such as pre-eclampsia claim their lives. Often it is the result of the appalling lack of skilled birth attendants, or a health post where corrupt officials have robbed the shelves of medicines. Many die because they are reluctant to journey to a health post because of a stigma, often perpetuated by other women, against delivering outside the village.

It is so important to educate them that in 10 per cent of births, complications that can kill may occur – and that is true around the world. It is not worth the risk.

This is the reason why the world sees some 500,000 women die from complications around childbirth each year – a sobering thought each Mother's Day.

The same is true to save their newborns lives. Simple things for making births at home safer, like immediately wrapping the baby up (as many die from hypothermia), wiping them down and breastfeeding as soon as possible, are life saving. Nearly 40 per cent of the 7.6 million children who annually die under the age of five die within the first month of life. In some villages in Laos children are not given a name until they are 12 months old. So many die there is no point. Most never get a birth or death certificate and the stillborn are not even recorded and would be millions more. Registration of birth and death even if stillborn is a human right – to say you were born and you existed. And contrary to our Western notions, a poor mother feels the same grief at the loss of a child as we do.

Those men have never carried a drop of water

I love watching the advertisements when charities devoutly declare that they are not political. What they mean to say, or in my view *should* say, is: we are not partisan but, of course, we are political.

We should never be partisan and have a secret agenda to back a particular political party or interfere in domestic politics – tempting as that is when dictators rule. But we cannot do development without being small 'p' political. Politics is about power and who gets what they want and who misses out. In Australia, a budget is simply the balance sheet of power and which special interest lobbyist won and who missed out.

Development and lifting people out of poverty often means disturbing power that is religiously and culturally enshrined in the status quo – think caste. And these power relations, left undisturbed, will continue to leave certain groups out because they have no power. If the power of moneylenders is not challenged, if the power of bureaucrats and politicians pilfering from the health and education budgets remains, if the power of big men at the local level is left to skew priorities away from community needs, there will be no development. Instead, we will continue to do a bit of charity – which is always needed, but becomes like pouring water into a bucket with a hole in it.

The largest group regularly left out are women. When we empower women, we are being highly political and we have an agenda. In highly patriarchal communities it is common for the women to do all the work. So to empower women is to subvert a culture, and that is touchy. It can have unintended consequences and upset power balances. But it is worth the risk. I cannot say how many times I have watched women toil in the fields or collect the water while the men sit and chat, drink tea and play card games. They would be surprised to be questioned about whether they loved their wives. 'Of course we do. Why would you even ask? But respect our culture where women are expected to do the heavy work.'

I have watched women on the border of Kenya and Somalia during that terrible drought draw water from the well that the World Vision water truck had just filled. After drawing water these women were struggling to stand upright with the weight of the water buckets on their heads while the men, thirty to forty of them, sat or stood and watched. The only finger lifted was when one man on one occasion stepped forward to help steady the bucket on a woman's head as she struggled to stand upright, straining with the wobbles of a weight-lifter moving from squat to press. That image has never left me.

* * *

Of course, men cannot be blamed for everything. Horizontal oppression is a term for when women hurt each other. In Zimbabwe after we conducted a gender audit, I listened with our staff in Harare to the results that included some amazing attitudes. Some Shona women will tell their daughters, in the time leading up to their wedding, that if their husband does not beat them in the first week of marriage, he probably does not love them. They tell their daughters they must never ask about what seed their husband chooses to grow. That is a man's domain. And when he goes off to market with the crop and comes back almost empty-handed with a likely story that he has been robbed, it is not for them to question. A good wife just does not do that.

These attitudes can spell a death sentence. If women who have reason to suspect their husbands' fidelity are not empowered to ask questions, or even to admit to and act on their suspicions, they can be infected with HIV. It is why I cannot accept the teaching that condoms are wrong and unacceptable to God. If a wife is not permitted to say to her husband that he will have to use a condom until he has an HIV test, the risk is that sex can be fatal for her and her family even though she has been faithful. But to even imagine that sort of change takes generations, and for that to even be a possibility, it requires the education of women and the empowerment of girls. We know that in every society it is largely women who regulate the behaviour of men. They must be allowed the tools and freedom to do so.

One of the best things we did after the crippling floods

that left nearly 20 million people homeless in Pakistan was set up women-only tents and spaces. The joy radiating from these communities was evident, as they had never experienced a women-only space in their village culture. The women's tent could hold over 200 and was set well apart. It was an amazing thing for them to be unburdened by the presence of men in a space where they could talk about health issues and pressures in their marriages, draw pictures and write lists of plans and what they wanted for their future in a rebuilt village. When they showed us their hopes, confidence exuded from them – the confidence of expressing their ideas without fear of transgressing norms. To see that level of excitement was a tonic. They had eminently smart and sensible plans for change and a new start. It was a free space where they processed feelings and talked with deep concern about the patterns of depression and pain they saw in their men. Floods had washed away their men's usefulness and dignity.

The men, by contrast, were curious and puzzled about this innovation. But they acknowledged that their wives were certainly happier and so, though they felt uncomfortable and were still unsure about the novel experiment, they reluctantly agreed it was better for them. Most acknowledged that because their villages and homes had been washed away, the women needed a place to regroup.

It was a start that could kindle an idea that may change basic cultural attitudes in the days to come. Change takes place slowly, but is best aided by beneficial outcomes for all concerned.

A modest proposal for peace

L est anyone think that empowering women is not controversial, let me tell you what happened to seven of our Pakistani staff in February 2007. We were one of the few aid agencies left in the region, as there had been threats from extremists. But the community and village elders assured us we could leave our protection to them. They wanted us to stay, as they needed our education and health work. Then came this assault of sickening ferocity.

On that fateful day, seven young, passionate Muslim World Vision staff members were executed in their office by extremists. One of our staff, with whom I talked later, is only alive today because he had walked out the back door to have a cigarette as the killers walked in the front entrance. The attack was heard on an open phone line to our headquarters in Islamabad, where our horrified staff heard the killers accuse the staff members of indecency. Indecency? All we could conclude was that it meant the attackers objected to our program for educating girls.

Around the world 40,000 people, mostly staff, mourned in a joint service conducted on six continents and prayed for the families of these courageous Muslim colleagues who loved their neighbours and paid the ultimate price for empowering women.

I reflected darkly on the murderous misfiring of extremist faith. In the war on terror, far more Muslims have been killed by other Muslims than by NATO's bombs or American drones. Just as in history, far more Christians have been killed by Christians than by any other group. Thinking of wars, from the Second World War to the dark troubles of Northern Ireland to the Rwandan genocide, in 1994 Stanley Hauerwas suggested what he called 'a modest proposal for peace'. It was: 'Let Christians of the world first agree to stop killing other Christians.' As I mourned, I prayed that Muslims would also adopt this modest proposal and at the very least stop killing other Muslims.

But I was also proud that World Vision, as a Christian humanitarian and development organisation, which started in 1950 in the US, chose to be in these dangerous places with Muslim staff showing the love of God. Far better to bomb with love and aid, than with the terrifying bombs of Western artillery that tear lives apart and intensify ideology and hatred.

Conny shows how

We have known for a long time that empowering women is the sharpest tool on the development rack. But I learned the hard way that the same is true of relief. You cannot do proper emergency relief without the leadership of women.

We were high up in the mountains of Pakistan a year after responding to a massive earthquake in 2008. After I badly twisted an ankle they found a donkey to carry me, so I arrived in the village, which was perched on a ravine, seated like the conquering Caesar on a donkey. My co-worker Conny had walked alongside me up the impossible inclines. Now Conny was excluded from the men-only gathering and sent off to find the women who were slaving in the back kitchens and cooking the feast for us.

I was embarrassed that she was excluded, but you have to be sensitive to culture. I hobbled off the donkey to the throne they provided for me, which was placed at the centre of a formal gathering of the social hierarchy, carefully arranged in pecking order. But it was all just the men. I was now wearing a glittering ceremonial turban they had placed on my head and was receiving lovely gifts and long speeches. The men all had long beards and were in their finest robes, their heads enthusiastically nodding in agreement at our great work. As I received gift after gift and basked in speech after speech of gratitude, I felt enormous pride at such a successful operation. So good to know our relief work was so well received.

I stumbled out laden with gifts and met Conny.

'It seems we have done a tremendous job here,' I began. She cut me down with one look. I asked what was wrong.

She said, 'I have been with the women and found out the real story. Because we asked the leaders – all men – where they wanted to place the new wells after their water supplies were compromised by the earthquake, those duffers told us all the wrong places.' I protested – surely, given that this was their village, they must know. Conny replied that they did not have a clue. As the women told her, the men had never carried a drop of water in their lives. How would they know?

I fell silent. Despite gifts and celebration, we had erred. Of course, when men are the gatekeepers to power and it is an emergency, it is a tricky negotiation. But we should have done much better.

The next day I watched Conny – a fiesty redhead – with hammer in hand, marching some of the bemused men down the valley and showing them how they could fix their damaged bridge themselves. The previous evening, flattered with their praise, I had shown sympathy for their request for someone to come and fix their bridge. But in the morning, Conny had it sorted.

'We should never do for people what they can do for themselves. Creating dependency is failure and we should find ways to start with the women, who are the least likely to be dependent!' Chastened, I found the strength to not need the donkey on the way back down!

One striking insight in Pakistan came about because of our worry that girls had to collect the clean water before going to school. As a consequence, many were not getting to school. A father always valued his sons' education before his daughters'. She could be a burden to raise and then just marry someone else and work for them. So the prospect of changing men's attitudes to educating their daughters is a long-range undertaking. There was a quicker way to get an outcome, and that was a deliberate engineering solution. We learnt to, wherever possible, place the taps and even the well near the school. That way the girls could do both!

An Australian treasure

D r Catherine Hamlin first went to Ethiopia in 1959. I visited the Addis Ababa Fistula Hospital, which she and her husband, Reg, founded, when I was on my trip to Ethiopia in 2009. Even after her husband, another obstetrician, was killed in a terrible car accident, Catherine stayed – and, at eight-five years of age, was still occasionally operating when I visited her.

Her whole life was handed over to the women of remote villages whose vaginas and bladders were irreparably torn in difficult childbirth. It meant that these women were rendered social and medical outcasts in a culture that despised uncleanness. The joy in the eyes of women whose lives were restored through an operation at the hospital was a wonder to behold. I was so proud to see the work that World Vision Australia had helped to support. And to meet the dignified Australian at the heart of it.

But I had first met Catherine in Melbourne a year or two earlier, when she asked to see me on one of her trips home. She insisted on calling me 'Reverend Costello', even though I asked that she call me Tim! She requested to meet with me at the Alexandria Club, a women's club in the city, where she was staying. In quaint old-world surrounds she poured tea, offered me cucumber sandwiches and spoke with such nobility and grace that I felt transported to purer times. She had studied medicine at Sydney University when few women were admitted to a male profession. With the world at her feet, she had chosen to dedicate her life to Ethiopian women facing a life sentence of stigma and disgust.

When I told Merridie I had been asked to meet Dr Catherine Hamlin, she insisted on coming with me. She had recently seen the documentary *A Walk to Beautiful*, which portrays the work of the hospital so poignantly. As it happened, Catherine sat for a while as we chatted, clasping Merridie's hands. Afterwards I was moved to hear Merridie say to a few friends that having her hands held by Catherine's hands – which had saved the dignity of so many women over the years – meant more to her than even having shaken hands with Bono. Now that's a big call, but shows the admiration Catherine inspires.

As I listened to her speak, I realised that she was a woman untouched by shallow affluence and careerism. She had completely missed the cynicism of our age and the slippage of civility and standards in the West as she buried herself for more than fifty years in Ethiopia. There was a beauty and incorruptibility about her. To me she seemed immune to the corrosion and self-seeking that characterises the last decades of economic growth and relentless materialism. Living selflessly was simple, and gave her moral and spiritual clarity. I felt that she spoke directly to my noblest self.

The search for the sacred

I took the actor Hugh Jackman and his actress wife, Deborra-Lee Furness, to look at some of World Vision's work in Ethiopia. One of my favourite moments was in Addis Ababa, the capital city. We watched in amazement as Ethiopians poured into churches to pray every morning and at many other times of the day. They take their faith very seriously.

They believe the actual Ark of the Covenant is housed in a small chapel in the town of Aksum in the northern highlands of Ethiopia. By actual I mean *actual*. Yes, the very Old Testament Ark where Jews believed the Holy One and Shekinah Glory of Yahweh actually lived. In the Ethiopian church the story is fervently believed that after the destruction of the city of Jerusalem and its glorious temple in 586 BC, the sacred Ark made its way to Ethiopia. So every church has a replica Ark enclosed and curtained off at its centre. And even that replica is so holy that a permanent barrier and shroud is built around it. For 80 million Ethiopians, housing this 'presence of God' in their nation is a sustaining belief and enhances their deep piety and discipline. We hoped we might get a glimpse of one of the replicas but knew that our chances would be slim.

We were at the church where Haile Selassie and other emperors were enthroned. A priest was giving us a guided tour of the many holy relics within the church and Hugh and I were vying for who might get to see the replica Ark. Hugh was splaying charm in every direction and had even, when asked where we came from, sang 'I still call Australia home' for the priest. I was doing my best to match him, but when it's Hugh Jackman performing, it is pretty stiff competition.

At the right moment, in a hushed voice imbued with religious deference and careful bonding, Hugh politely asked if the priest could take him up the steps and behind the curtains and unlock the enclosure, so he could glimpse the Ark and pay due worship. The priest was unmoved and firmly refused, explaining that it was a privilege only for priests. Not even the Ethiopian devout were allowed that right.

Hugh was crestfallen, but I saw my opportunity. I jumped in and told him I was a priest. He looked astonished, but the others (even Hugh) assured him that indeed I was a priest from Australia. Somewhat surprised, he relaxed and, looking at me intently, said, 'Well then, you can come.' As I mounted the steps with him, I turned and gave the others the thumbs up. It felt like I would triumph at the Raider-of-the-Lost-Ark challenge.

At the top of the stairs, as he took out his keys, the priest turned and quietly repeated, 'Are you really a priest?' I truthfully nodded. Then came the question that sunk me. 'And you are a priest of the Orthodox Church?'

Pinned. I squeaked out, 'No, the … Baptist Church.' He snapped the keys back in his pocket and marched back down the steps, with me limping behind. So close, but yet so far from the sacred.

I have felt the same anticipation in other places of historic sacred significance: the magnificent Hagia Sophia in Istanbul, St Peter's Basilica in Rome, the Church of the Nativity in Bethlehem, the Shwedagon Buddhist temple in Yangon and the Faisal Mosque in Islamabad to name but a few. But I have felt the same disappointment that my experience of the sacred was never commensurate with my anticipation, given the significance of these sites.

Yet in places most pedestrian and poor, and where it is least expected, I have at times been overwhelmed with awe at the sense of the presence of something greater. Being taken by surprise is almost always the universal element in the experience of God and grace for me.

Ducale

Hugh, Deb and I were driven five hours south of Addis into the coffee-farming district. This is an ancient area where coffee was first cultivated 3000 years ago. But the farmers there are poor and 90 per cent of the trees are gone – cut down for firewood, the only source of fuel and energy for cooking. Of course, it is the women who must collect the firewood and, because of the scarcity of trees, they are venturing further from home to find timber. Their long journeys exacerbate their risk of injury, rape and even abduction. The farmers' cottages have thatched roofs and no chimney or windows. On the trip down, we saw smoke leaching through the thatched roofs of the cottages. The fires that burn in the centre of the homes, providing light and heat for cooking, also give respiratory illnesses to the children inside.

World Vision had provided some of the farmers with a methane digester. A simple trap to be placed over the rubbish-and-manure pit, it captures the methane produced from the waste and then pipes it into the hut. Immediately the family is cooking on gas, eliminating the need to cut down trees and breathe in smoke, and the women are no longer putting themselves at risk travelling huge distances to collect wood.

For a few hours, Hugh stripped down and toiled with a farmer called Ducale. They wheeled rubbish into his manure pit, patting it down with a spade as they did so. All of this was done by Hugh in his Gucci boots, mind. Ducale did not speak a word of English and had no idea who Hugh was.

I watched as later they sat having a coffee together in Ducale's hut holding hands, laughing and hugging – all without a word in common. Thanks to the methane digester, Ducale has opened a coffee shop in his hut and has become an energy exporter to the village. His income has skyrocketed, his children get to study by smokeless gaslight at night, and they are doing better at school. As Hugh and Ducale sat and drank coffee together after their sweaty work, I learned that physical work transcends words and culture.

Hugh and Deb planted two coffee trees at the back of Ducale's hut and named them after their kids, Oscar and Eva. They promised to bring them to visit Ducale's farm in a few years. Two families separated by global extremes, celebrating joy and family.

Hope always springs into my mind whenever I smell coffee.

Alok Tochs

I have been doing a bit of work with the Sudanese community in Melbourne. In 2011, refugees from Africa's longest civil war rejoiced at seeing South Sudan at last win independence and become the world's newest nation.

But South Sudan still has the least infrastructure of any nation in Africa, and it will be a long journey to overcome the tribal conflicts that could cripple the new nation. In a few states, the tribal wars are already threatening to devour their unity. For the Sudanese refugees, it is also a striking challenge to come from the least advanced and most remote corner of Africa and make a new life in the cities of the West. For parents desperate to inculcate their children with community traditions, there are many adjustments to make.

Australian teachers know that teaching Sudanese children English, when their parents at home cannot read or write, requires teaching the parents too. It is a huge task. They must explain Australian culture to the families; men must learn that beating their wives and children, while acceptable in Sudan, is considered assault here. Teachers are mandated to report children who come to school with obvious bruises, and when the police are involved there is bewilderment and anger from the men. Our rules or theirs? It is a clash of civilisations.

Likewise, a big man is expected to have more than one wife, and many make visits home to take a second wife. Even the educated Sudanese women in Melbourne justify this: as the civil war meant that there were far more women than men, they argue that polygyny (the practice of having more than one wife at a time) made sense. For a woman not to have a chance to have children due to the lack of available men would be the far greater shame.

But one of the more remarkable cultural traditions that I have stumbled upon in my meetings with the Sudanese is called 'Alok Toch'. It is a party thrown by the wife's family, who give the husband gifts of money and a feast. Hundreds attend an Alok Toch, and the high moment is to watch the wife feed her husband with a spoon of food and hold up a glass of milk and pour it down his throat.

Until the wife's family throws an Alok Toch, the husband's social life is restricted. He cannot eat or drink (or even go to the toilet) at any meal or party hosted by a member of the wife's family. He attends events, but cannot participate because it is disrespectful to the family. He must wait until offered an Alok Toch, which is totally at the discretion of the wife's family.

The Alok Toch I attended was ten years after the wedding and three children later. There were many speeches, dancing and, of course, the ritual with the milk. But all I could think was: what had this man done wrong, to be made to wait ten years before he could eat at the family's festive dinners?

Perhaps the culture had to build in an equalising exercise of power for the wife's family to place constraints on the husband – a family probation to make sure he treated her right. I like that as, to my mind, there needs to be something done to balance the scales in terms of power. When a girl marries in this culture she is usually still in her teens, and is hitched to a guy up to twenty-five years older. It is her uncles who do the negotiations on the behalf of her parents. They bargain with the man or his family about the number of cows (or in Australia, the amount of dollars) she is worth. If she is tall and has a gap in her teeth (both very sought-after traits), comes from a good family and has some education, then she is worth more. The idea is that her family must be paid a fair price for feeding and educating her, as now she will leave and work for another man. At least an Alok Toch goes some way towards redresses the power imbalance.

I am still waiting for my wife's family to give me an Alok Toch after thirty-three years of marriage!

When they said I was fat

ugh Jackman and Daniel Craig performed a wonderful two-man play on Broadway. It happened to be on when I was in New York for a conference with the UN for the Millennium Development Goals. Hugh sent through some tickets for me and my daughter Claire, who was there with me, and told us to come backstage and catch him after. So, of course, we did.

There I was, in a dressing room with a couple of others, including a face I vaguely recognised but could not place. I noticed my daughter was somewhat in awe and lost for words as I made some small talk with this self-assured older woman. At that point Hugh bounded in, hugged me and said 'Now Tim, have you met Barbara Walters?' So *that* was the face I could not place. Oh dear, my bad memory! And my daughter's embarrassment! Afterwards, she made sure I heard about my faux pas for quite some time. In the heat of the moment, I failed to tell Barbara of an interview she did that had stayed in my mind as a parable of the personal and political.

It was her interview with Monica Lewinsky, right after Bill Clinton had finally beaten impeachment. Despite his victory, the man and the office once revered throughout the world had taken an extraordinary battering. For months the world had been transfixed by every turn and twist of the proceedings. But now, the months of dangerous political paralysis at the heart of the American government were finally over, and Monica was giving her first interview. Barbara asked her what, of all the millions of words written and thousands of images published, what had hurt her the most. She replied, 'When they said I was fat.'

So that was the crux of it? The world's most powerful man had nearly fallen – the government of the world's only superpower had been perilously frozen. But the real issue for Monica was as basic as the way every man and woman feels when they look at their own body-shape in the mirror and wish it to be better? The sorely personal is the lens through which most of us look at even grave issues. To underestimate those feelings is to be blindsided.

One postscript to the Bill and Monica saga. I was rung by the Australian media in my capacity as President of the Baptist Union of Churches in Australia, which I was at that time. The call came immediately after Bill had solemnly sworn on TV, 'I did not have sexual relations with that woman.' The press here in Australia knew that Bill was a Baptist. Their nuanced question to me was 'So, is it true in Baptist theology that oral sex does not constitute sexual relations?'

I answered, 'Now there's a question I have no memory being canvassed by our teachers in seminary.'

An American phenomenon

Some years ago, I was addressing staff at the World Vision US headquarters in Seattle. I spoke of my deep admiration for the American achievement.

'In times when the world only knew of the divine right of kings, a state church that persecuted nonconformists and where aristocrats and entrenched social classes ruled, the American bill of rights declared this truth to be self evident: that all men are born equal. What a statement of astonishing and breathtaking freedom. To declare, against the known hierarchical order in Europe, a republican sentiment ("We the People ...") was a historical breakthrough that has changed the story of mankind,' my talk went. 'The American Revolution was maybe the first revolution in history that did not devour its own children.' I finished off by explaining that this was why I am proud to call myself a republican (as opposed to a monarchist).

I was amazed, at the end of my talk, how many staff came up to me and thanked me, saying 'that was wonderful' and 'I am a Republican too, and voted for George W. Bush'. I had to quickly spell it out that I actually meant small 'r' republican.

Even God-fearing believers like me find it curious that every American presidential candidate finds it compulsory to invoke God and faith in public electioneering. Maybe that is because I have always admired the sentiments of the Reformer Martin Luther's adage: 'Give me a wise Turk [Muslim] rather than a foolish Christian to rule over us.'

But it is not just the personal faith biography of candidates, and mandatory final line of every speech (God Bless America) that I find a little odd. It is the national default setting that seems to have an American flag wrapped around the Christian cross that puzzles me as a Christian.

At the time of writing, Newt Gingrich had given his speech after winning a Republican Primary in South Carolina. He said the forthcoming presidential election was between American exceptionalism and Saul Alinsky, a Chicago activist – it was a veiled reference to Obama and socialism.

Mitt Romney, the Republican presidential contender agreed and charged President Obama with a failure to believe in American exceptionalism. This forced the President to assert that he did believe in it.

So American exceptionalism or the special relationship between God and America is now up for election or under threat from Obama?

The concept of American exceptionalism is this: it is the God-given destiny of America to not just demonstrate freedom, but be the definition of God's freedom in the world. The US chooses to not be subject to the International Criminal court and some other conventions such as the Rights of the Child because of this exceptional streak. Presumably this is why all their leaders seem required to remind us that the US is the greatest nation on earth. Maybe true, but it is said so often to remind us that something deeper and exceptional is present. This exceptionalism is grounded in the Christian vision from pilgrim father John Winthrop at Massachusetts Bay, speaking of the fledgling settlement being a city on a hill and a light in a dark place. America has since believed that among the nations of the world it has a manifest destiny born in a special covenant relationship with God. It is to be exceptional. It is strongly alive today with Republican candidates. It rears its head in every presidential election.

I was reminded of the words of former president George H. Bush in finishing a speech in Texas for the 1982 presidential campaign. He concluded with, 'Did not Jesus himself teach that America is to be a light to the nations?' The audience wildly applauded.

I am still trying to locate that verse in my New Testament.

Obama and the planet

I t is for Americans, not for me, to pontificate on Obama's presidency and the value of his politics and policies. But given that American power in the world is like the sun, whose rays reach us all, let me reflect on what I observed at a state dinner I attended in his honour in our Parliamentary Great Hall in Canberra in November 2011.

The excitement was palpable. Every detail of the menus, dress code and invitee list was carefully managed. No invitee who I know of missed the opportunity to be there.

As I listened to President Obama tease us with mock attempts at an Australian accent and Aussie colloquialisms, people sat in spellbound attention. He went on to address the sustained US–Australian ties through war and peace. Some of this awe directed at him was the celebrity syndrome that puts brains into neutral. But his speech was substantial and went deeper. I realised that he had a true gift – the ability to make us feel good about who we are and what we have achieved.

Here was the most powerful man in the world, addressing our anxieties about our place in the world like a powerful big brother, saying we were mates and wc were okay in the eyes of the US. His presence alone soothed our need for significance. It was declared that we would have a joint US–Australia military base in Darwin. He didn't say 'because you feel exposed'. But it certainly was implied.

As a nation, we are well off Broadway (only on the way to Antarctica), with a population of just 22 million. We define ourselves as a multicultural nation, but experience periodic outbreaks of anxiety about that term because our institutions and inclinations are essentially those of a European nation. Some Australians' inner fear, represented by the regular arrival of boats of refugees, is that they may find themselves, as European descendants, in the wrong neighbourhood – an Asian neighbourhood. One of our nearest neighbours is Indonesia, which is the largest Muslim nation in the world. My grandparents were of English, Scottish and Irish stock. I noticed, when staying with them, that they threw open the curtains in the kitchen in the morning, looked out and just maybe wished that they might see London, Edinburgh or Dublin in the distance, not Dili, Port Moresby or Jakarta.

Americans may not understand the importance of this role in a president when he visits allies like us. I watched with fascination what happened in the Great Hall after his speech. When it became apparent that Obama would not move around to all the tables, suddenly politicians and members of Australia's power clique rose from their seats and started to stream in his direction.

I watched as anti-American-alliance Greens, Labor members of the Socialist Left and Tory-type conservative politicians alike rushed towards his table. These were our leaders – otherwise dignified politicians with status and poise. As I overheard one Green MP say as the fast-massing queue came past my table, 'I know it is embarrassing but I just have to try and touch him.'

I turned to our former prime minister, John Howard, who was standing discreetly beside me. I asked him if he had ever seen anything like it. He smiled and shook his head in disbelief.

* * *

When it comes to this phenomenon, I think Obama's life story is the best explanation. Here is an American president with a half-sister who is Indonesian, who spent some years growing up in Muslim Indonesia: the country at our nation's front door and, as the largest Muslim nation in the world, a source of continuing Australian misunderstanding and misgiving. He is a black man in the White House. He had a Kenyan grandmother from a humble village, and a Muslim African father. As he showed in his Cairo address, he can use that pedigree to say some tough things about human rights and still get a hearing in the Arab world. Raised by a single white mum, he was able to transcend parochialism and be global in sympathy and identity. It may explain to Americans why the man, so unpopular at times at home, is so loved internationally.

Being small and off Broadway, we in Australia know that the world is a waterbed. Press down in one place, and something comes up elsewhere. We join the American effort in going to war in Iraq, and eighty-eight Australians die on holiday in Bali through a payback bomb blast. Swine flu breaks out in Mexico, and we are closing primary schools in Melbourne. Banks with funny names that few Australians had ever heard of – Fannie Mae and Freddie Mac – get into trouble in the US, and our economy and banking system, along with those the world over, are hit.

Intuitively, we know we need a US president with a global sensitivity and a global perspective. I think that somehow gives the rest of us in the free world all the opportunity to have some audacity to hope.

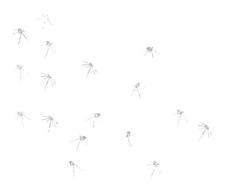

A dream when down

I have kept a journal for much of the last forty years. On 8 January 1986, I wrote about feeling somewhat depressed and lacking in vision. I was reflecting on finishing my first fifteen months as a Baptist minister in St Kilda, an inner-suburban bayside suburb of Melbourne. It was an area known for street prostitution, drug addiction and homelessness, but also an enclave of wealthy people in mansions on St Kilda hill, so there was an extraordinary range of social, economic and moral challenges there. My ideals and hopes had met the hard reality of broken and confused lives. I was tired and dispirited.

On the evening of the next day, Merridie and I watched a TV program on the life of Martin Luther King. It finished with his famous 'I have a dream' speech given in Washington at the 1963 Civil Rights March. I wrote later in my journal how the speech pierced my depression – I felt charged with a fresh hope and purpose, simply by the power of those words:

I have a dream that my four little children will one day
    live in a nation
where they will not be judged by the colour of their skin,
but by the content of their character.

Within an hour of watching the show Merridie was in labour, and the next morning our third child, a son, was born. There was no debate about him being called Martin, after Dr King, himself a Baptist minister who never gave up in the face of huge pressures and impossible odds.

Years later I heard more of the story of this speech (which, in my opinion, is the greatest piece of oration of the twentieth century). The story goes that Dr King had given much of this same speech in Chicago some months earlier at the church of Reverend Franklin. The Reverend's nineteen-year-old daughter Aretha had sung a solo in the church that night. She was then also part of the stage crowd at the Washington Mall when Dr King delivered the speech we are all now familiar with. Dr King was speaking from some notes and only just barely into the speech when Aretha called out to him, 'Tell them about your dream, Martin!'

He heard her words, nodded, paused and put the script aside. Martin Luther King's voice changed and he lifted his face as he moved into this soaring speech. This dream had inspired Aretha; that day it electrified the Washington Mall and, in totally different circumstances over twenty years later, it broke through to me.

It continues to touch others in similar ways. I was in a Sunday service in October 2011 at Shiloh Baptist Church in East Harlem on the morning President Obama was to open the Martin Luther King commemorative statue on the Washington Mall. The emotion in the church became charged as they remembered 'Brother Martin'

and how he changed their lives. I will never forget 'The
Battle Hymn of the Republic' being sung and lines from
a latter verse repeated over and over until I was almost
in a trance. Words that spoke of the Christ that Dr King
followed: 'As he died to make men holy, so we live to set
men free. His truth is marching on.'

Yes, here was the dream lifting me again.

I have a dream that one day on the red hills of Georgia,
the sons of former slaves and the sons of former slave
    owners
will be able to sit together at the table of brotherhood.

Better than I used to be

Black music has always stirred something in me. It is music that is born in suffering. The spirituals emerged from slavery. We speak today of slavery to drugs, drink or gambling. We understand an addiction as that which consumes the life of the sufferer. But human slavery was an addiction of legally sanctioned evil. A master lawfully consumed the life of another human. A master literally took over the lives of his slaves and their families and consumed their hopes and very existence – not according to their needs, but to his. Legally, the slaves only existed for someone else. To sing when in such chains was to literally call up hope from the bowels of evil and despair.

When I first heard The Blind Boys of Alabama perform live in Melbourne, I was transported to the fields of the American south. Even today, with slavery abolished and civil rights won, I realised that if you are black and blind and from the south like Alabama, you are still starting way behind. Yet music and spirituals are still the consolation and source for hope or, in The Blind Boys' case, musical achievement.

The song that touched me that night was called 'I'm getting better all the time'. There is a line in the chorus:

'I am not what I oughta be, but I am better than I used to be'. Why did it move me? Maybe it was because I have been born into a religious tradition with a strong streak of perfectionism – called holiness. Truthfully, trying to be holy is crippling because the bar is way too high. I have learnt that expectations in life are important because if they are too low, we do not strive to do better. If they are too high, we feel crushed and give up. Managing expectations appropriately seems to be the great trick in getting life right.

To hear The Blind Boys catch in one musical refrain both a realistic and, for me, a perfect pitch of expectations was wonderful. It acknowledges the need to keep trying but also to accept failures. This was soul soothing. And, coming from them, it resonated with the legacy of centuries of suffering and gave me hope. So I can go on knowing I am certainly not what I ought to be, but still I am better than I used to be. And that is enough for the moment.

Horizons

My good friend Grant, who is Aboriginal, was driving on the highway with his young son William in the backseat. The billboards lining the road were advertising the latest-model car, showing the happy people who owned them and drove them.

William asked Grant how come it was only white fellas who drove those cars in the advertisements. Grant replied, 'Well, how many of our Aboriginal mob do you ever see driving nice cars, son? That's why.'

William said, 'Yeah, but what about Uncle Tim? He has a nice car.'

Grant laughed and said, 'What do you mean?'

William said, 'He's one of our mob, isn't he?'

Hearing that story, I felt honoured. William had seen our quality of friendship and the good times together – the tone of my skin had not occurred to him.

I am not Aboriginal, but after four years of study in Switzerland I noticed I felt oddly depressed. I just wanted to get home, and attributed the feelings to homesickness. I missed the untidiness of the Australian landscapes, compared to the chocolate-box perfection and beauty of Switzerland. Charles Darwin, on his visit to Australia, called it the untidiest natural terrain he had ever seen. But to me that was home. I missed our sprawling cities, in contrast with the precision of Swiss culture. I even longed for a train that ran late – something impossible in Swiss transport.

But it wasn't until I got home that I realised what it was that I most missed. It was horizons: of land and sky, of sea and sky. I had felt closed in by the mountainous and landlocked country where I had spent almost four years studying. I did not know why I immediately rushed to the beach when I got home. Until I saw that horizon, I would never have connected feelings of depression to the lack of it. Every time I see that straight line where sea and sky meet, or a vast expanse of Australia's plains, I feel elated. Most holidays I take are in the bush, or involve walking by the sea to just soak in the pencil line so far off. It lifts my vision and I start dreaming. Horizons for me are the key to renewing the dream.

Part of the mantra of every parent and teacher is to tell their kids to dream big or to follow their dreams. Even people living in prisons of poverty, like rural landless families in Asia and Africa trying to survive on less than two dollars a day, even their children have dreams. The most direct question I always ask kids is, 'What do you want to be when you grow up?' When asked, the children's faces light up with hopeful smiles. The answers are rarely to be a farmer like Dad, but rather a pilot, a doctor, a teacher, a policeman or president. I think they have certainly dreamed big. How will they ever get there when the teachers, who are not paid regularly, fail to turn up? How will they get there if, when they get to school, many struggle to concentrate because they have walked so far and suffer often with terrible nutrition?

Even against odds like these, a dream can unlock seemingly impossible chances. In 2010, I got to visit a child that our family has sponsored for some years. I was fortunate as some 400,000 Australians sponsor children by giving an amount each month for someone they will never met. In my case, I met a young girl, nine years old, called Tatenda in Zimbabwe. To see a bright little girl in person whose face peers at me from my fridge door was deeply moving. I met her and her proud family and saw the delight in their eyes at the opportunities education was bringing to their daughter and the children in the village. Tatenda's dream is to be a teacher. Like her, so many children around the world are getting opportunities for aspiration.

Teriano from the Maasai culture in Kenya is another such story. I visited the Maasai some years ago – magnificent and proud people that they are. Teriano was the eldest of fifteen children in a culture where girls marry early. Due to World Vision sponsorship and the support of her parents, who defied the customs, she got through her schooling and was accepted into college where she trained as a community worker. Now she is studying social work on a scholarship in Canada. She is determined to go back to her own village and help her people adapt to the changing world, especially by embracing the potential of girls and women. In her own words: 'I love being Maasai, but I am also an educated woman. I know I can be both.'

In remote Aboriginal communities I have asked the same question. The boys, when asked what they want to be, universally answer: a League footballer. It is not a bad answer, as professional football is one area where Aboriginals are massively over-represented as a percentage of the population. At the highest professional level of Australian Rules football there are some 13 per cent who are Aboriginal players earning the big money compared to their 1.5 per cent of the national population. Their genius on the field has led to speculation that the prototype of Australian Rules football was a pre-European Aboriginal game played with a possum fur rolled into a ball. In central Australia it was a ball of emu feathers tied together with string made of human hair. But still, making the grade is very long odds. For every success, there are thousands of others who do not realise this dream. Sadly, rejection and disappointment and the lack of other opportunities can lead to a ruined life, which unfortunately can revolve around welfare dependency, petrol sniffing and alcoholism. How do you refashion a passionate but unachieved dream?

But perhaps to not dream is infinitely worse. It is the very definition of depression and a collapsed horizon.

* * *

A few years ago, I took some of our Australian Football League stars to visit our projects in South Africa. One of them was Aboriginal football star Nathan Lovett-Murray. He was inspired by the hope of black people who had suffered, and was bowled over that there were so many of them! They were a majority in their own country. They had culture, language and pride. He knew of the suffering in his Aboriginal community, being caught between cultures as a minority in Australia. It made me realised anew just how hard it is to be a black minority in our nation.

As we sat in the suburban Johannesburg home of Chabelli, our urbane national director, Nathan's eyes grew bigger upon hearing of the local cultural practices. We heard how, before his wedding, Chabelli took off his suit and, behind his carport, slaughtered a beast and proceeded to carve the carcass up in exactly the right manner. All right there in suburbia. It was cultural preparation within his community, to demonstrate that he was ready to marry. Culture is strong.

These footballers are tough and among the fittest sport stars in the world. They play a high-contact game without helmets or shoulder pads. But there in South Africa, they were often in tears, but not just at the poverty and struggle. Mornings with World Vision staff began with singing and dancing and prayer. It moved them deeply to see such joy, and they kept saying that they had never experienced anything like that as preparation for the day.

Some Aussie Rules football is played by black teams in the South African townships. National rugby and cricket has been historically white. The players whom

I was accompanying took some of the local kids for Aussie Rules training and then coached the teams in a competitive match. One of our guys gave a typical Australian coach's pre-match address to his side about hitting their opponent hard and keeping possession of the ball. I could see it all falling a bit flat in that context.

The other side's coach took a different tack. He said to his team, 'Rather than having me speak before the game, you boys tell me what inspires you.' Back came the answer from the team that they loved singing and dancing. So he led them onto the field with the players singing and dancing. He finished in the centre of the field, the team of kids encircling him with wide eyes. And he finished with, 'Go and play; be as strong as a lion.'

You guessed it – yes, they won the game. By an African mile.

A rabbit-proof fence

One of the most remarkable stories in Australian history is immortalised now in a film called *Rabbit-proof Fence*. It is based on a true story about three young mixed-race Aboriginal girls, aged between ten and thirteen, who in 1931 escaped from the Moore River Native Settlement (near Perth) where they had been placed after being removed from their Aboriginal parents in Jigalong, some 2400 kilometres away to the north.

This was at a time when the government was determined to breed out the colour of Aboriginal kids and 'save' those with some white blood from the degradations of Aboriginal bush life. These young girls not only escaped from the settlement but travelled on foot back home, guided by following the rabbit-proof fence that stretched across half the continent and incidentally never kept the rabbits or foxes out. One of the great follies of our history.

My interest in this story began with my Aunt Frances, an Anglican deaconess whose colleague and companion was Sister Eileen Heath. Both dedicated their lives to serving Australia's Indigenous peoples in and around Alice Springs in Central Australia. These people are the descendants of forebears who arrived here 40,000 years ago, making them the oldest living society anywhere in the world.

Aunt Frances and Sister Eileen's lives were models of dedication and faith. Both taught me patience in wanting to 'solve' the challenge of Aboriginal disadvantage. Sister Eileen died in 2011 at the age of 104. Until well after her hundredth birthday, she was still writing letters to Aboriginal friends – many of them today's leaders whom she had taught and adored. Every morning she prayed for them.

I visited Eileen in a nursing home in Perth just before I was heading up to Jigalong in 2010. I told Eileen I was visiting some of the work World Vision supports with the Aboriginal community there. I knew it was the area that the three Aboriginal girls walked home to, along the rabbit-proof fence, and whose story the film had made famous. Eileen, then approaching 103 years of age, said, 'Well if you are there, please give my love to Daisy. I think she is the only one of the three left.' I was taken aback and asked her how she knew Daisy and she said, 'Oh, I was the Sister-in-Charge at Moore River when the girls were there in the 1930s.' Sure enough, when I got to Jigalong I found Daisy sitting outside her humpy in the red dust. She was now eighty-five, and nearly blind. I gave her Eileen's greetings and love. She smiled a broad smile and said she loved Eileen and sure remembered her.

I was struck with this arc of complex and conflicted history. The missionaries were blamed for so much of the damage to Indigenous culture. They sent the children to Sunday school, required English to be learnt, clothes to be worn and industry to be taught. How colonial and culturally insensitive that would be deemed now. But here in Eileen was one of those missionaries who stayed and learnt the local languages. And who was deeply loved. I would read the letters from her 'kids' who were now all over the nation. I would laugh at the stories she told. Like how Charlie Perkins, later a leader of the 1960s Aboriginal Freedom ride, wrote in his biography that he was born in the bush with little care. Eileen read that and immediately wrote to him, telling him, 'No, Charlie, you were born in Alice Springs Base Hospital. I was there.' Charlie changed the story in the next edition. He knew Sister Eileen was not one whose word you could disregard.

Of course, the missionaries were people of their times, with the flaws of those times. But is that not true of all of us? And even more devastating, given our judgemental attribution of all the mistakes of the times to them? Having blamed the missionaries and removed church paternalism, we may be stunningly blind to our own failures. We have now had two generations of 'secular and socially enlightened' fly in, fly out technocrats. In fact, so many that whenever a community hears the growl of a four-wheel drive arriving with more well-intentioned experts ready to consult, they go fishing or hunting. At least in contrast the missionaries stayed, learnt the language and formed deep relationships, unlike the revolving door of multiple bureaucrats all armed with a consultation and empowerment manual. Eileen stayed forty years in Alice Springs on a tiny church stipend, serving Aboriginal people and enjoying true friendships and respectful relationships.

Yes, we have recently instituted land rights and sought reconciliation – both very good things. Yet on every social indicator, from health and life expectancy to education and domestic violence, the picture is worse and 'closing the gap' between mainstream Australia and Indigenous Australia is becoming harder to do. On the misery index, Indigenous disadvantage soars despite billions of dollars spent on the back of such enlightened policies. The common lament is that the best-educated and most able Aboriginal leaders still come from the missionary generations.

Jigalong was remarkable, not just for the rabbit-proof fence saga. It was the camp township where the last Aboriginal desert community, who had never seen white men, walked out of the bush. They entered Jigalong in the 1970s. Speaking with a daughter of one of these men, she described how amazing her father was, jumping the centuries to adapt. Everything for him was utterly different in culture and conception to his traditional dreaming. I felt listening to her describe him that I was connecting to a totally parallel universe.

My Granny Smith

I cannot walk the streets of St Kilda today without seeing the shadow of Eva Briggs. She was an Aboriginal street person who was the Mother Teresa of the streets. Though she suffered from a mental illness, I have never met someone who took her Christian faith so genuinely, loved everyone and gave away even her last few dollars to whoever was in need.

She died at fifty-two after having a heart attack in the street. Sadly, it was before she could meet her natural daughter who she had adopted out as a baby. She often spoke to me about this daughter and wondered aloud if she would be doing okay. This daughter received word of Eva's death from her adoptive mother, and so she turned up at my church in St Kilda one Sunday evening soon after Eva died. At the conclusion of the service she stood with a girlfriend at the door until others had left. Then quietly she began her story with tears in her eyes. 'I believe you knew my mother …'

Eva's daughter was now a married woman with three children of her own. She was a fine Christian, and she was a music teacher. My eyes moistened as I thought of Eva's gift for playing piano and how she would sit down and thump out by ear 'Amazing Grace' after our services. Eva's prayers for this, her only child, had been answered. To me it felt such a tragedy of timing. How much they could have meant to each other – but alas it was not to be, due to her untimely death.

Eva taught me, the one with the theological degrees, what it was to believe and live the Gospel. Faith was as natural to her as breathing. She knew God loved her despite the terrible circumstances she had lived through, including an unplanned pregnancy and having a child out of wedlock. She knew she was a loved child of God despite the mental illness that had caused her periods of distress. And she lived a life that expressed love and service.

I will never forget Eva's funeral. Upon her death, we discovered the Sacred Heart Catholic Church was also a spiritual home for her. So the priest there and I shared the service in his large church. It was almost full, and the faces were mainly of St Kilda's street folk – with not a dry eye in sight. They all knew her. They all loved her. They all knew she struggled like them but would never turn them away in need. Eva would always say, 'Bless you, love.' And mean it.

Australians as a whole have few pretensions. It probably comes from European settlement, starting as a British prison with the convict trash and the unwanted as our ancestors. As a nation, our only use was to solve the problem of Britain's overcrowded prisons. We may have joked that we were chosen by the best judges in England, but the stain was still there. But every society has its conceits, however humble its origins may be.

We still find ways to create a stock of our own airs and graces. So it is people from the edge (often Indigenous) like Eva who continue to surprise and expose them when we get haughty.

It is why I love the old Australian story of Granny Smith. She was a battler in the mid-1800s caring for her family on an orchard on the outskirts of Sydney. Tired from cooking for so many, one day she scooped up seeds and skins of apples in her apron and just threw them out at the back of the block. A year later she noticed a small apple tree growing. Within a few years, it was producing a new type of juicy apple then unknown. Today we call it the Granny Smith apple. Reputedly she said, 'Isn't it amazing – what man rejects, God uses to make something beautiful.' It is a parable of a nation that began with discards that has made good. As the joke goes, a nation whose forbears were chosen by the best judges in England.

Eva was my Granny Smith.

What? And plunge the
world into total darkness?

I often tell a story (maybe apocryphal) of the Hopi
Native Americans, who inhabit the mesas (cut-off
plateau mountains) of north-eastern Arizona in the
US. For millennia, they have been rising before dawn
on their flat mountains and praying the sun up. Of
course, it is an ancient set of rituals and prayers, but the
effect for their belief system is to see the sun rise.

The four important elements in the definition of
an ancient group today are elders, tribal land, rituals
and at least five anthropologists studying them! Some
anthropologists were camped with the Hopi, researching
and watching them. One of the anthropologists came
up with a suggestion. 'Why don't you just sleep in one
morning? Don't do your ritual and prayers. Just roll over
and go back to sleep.' The elders discussed this, came to
a quick consensus and came back and flatly refused. The
researcher said, 'But one morning would not make that
much difference, would it?'

They shot back the answer, 'What, and plunge the
world into total darkness for the sake of your stupid
experiment?'

We give a knowing smile when we hear this story, but

who is right? Science may be on our side, but once the sun rises without their prayers, a whole culture and way of life drifts apart. The darkness would be real, if not physical. Their whole sense of purpose and daily routine would be shattered.

It is fundamentally a political act to question the power structures in a culture. Many would question by what right we do this – is this not covert colonialism under the guise of the twenty-first century notion of development? Aid and free markets may be a softer form than guns and empire administrators, but they are equally effective in subjugating other cultures to a Western worldview.

We do need to be self-critical about the blindness of our superior insights. They may be just as real and no different to the same conceits of past generations we deplore. Even when we learn the language, adopt the dress and mores, we can never fully inhabit the cultural story of others and know better. They are different and have a right to be different.

But there are some fundamental questions where we have to chance our arm and allow that we might get it wrong. I prefer to chance my arm than to bow to those relativists who say there are no universal human rights, only Western conceptions that are different to African or Asian conceptions of human rights. Their take on it would mean we fold up any efforts to help, and retire to our cultural corner without the confidence to act.

This will be an eternal debate. In the West we value individual freedoms of speech, assembly and religion, whereas others value social rights like a job and housing, and find individual rights expendable as long as these are met. Development must be offering the good life as people choose to name it for themselves. But that is a key point, as we can get one-sided versions of the good life with little choice. An example of this is China demanding no criticism or interference in its domestic arrangements, which make political freedoms dispensable. The Chinese economic miracle is their showcase of development, and it has lifted millions out of poverty. But if you are Tibetan or Uyghur, you may wonder at the price. The same debate is played out about suspending the rights of terrorists, subjecting them to water-boarding and rendition to nations that have the stomach for torture. Does collective national security override absolute and universal human rights? Who decides when it is lawful if the courts have their jurisdiction removed?

We have this debate within Australia. Should tribal ways of payback justice, that include spearing and assault, be permitted, given they are a 40,000-year-old culture's method and still accepted as remedial justice? Should young girls be permitted to effectively be forced into marriages to older men because of an ancient culture? How do we reconcile that as a nation, when we have signed international treaties about respecting culture and difference and forbidding such summary justice for any citizen?

The Commonwealth Government's military and bureaucratic intervention into remote Aboriginal communities, starting in 2008, was to protect human rights after the 'Little Children Are Sacred' report revealed unacceptable levels of child abuse. But what did it do for the culture and self-sufficiency of the communities? And did it leave Aboriginal men in general stigmatised as child abusers? If the intervention had been explained on the basis of poverty, not race, could stigma against Aboriginal men have been avoided?

Cultures are never stationary and must accommodate new intermarriages, idioms, laws and beliefs. I believe that the power deficit of children and women is so obvious that challenging cultures who want to fudge these rights in the name of a traditional way of life is worth the risk. Better to risk damage trying to protect children and give them a future than condemn them to the vagaries of a museum view of a static and ancient culture.

Kill them cleanly

I remember spending a morning with some of Australia's army generals. I was asked to speak on ethics. I was amazed at how well-read and sophisticated these men were. Their grasp of international issues and geopolitical strategies was striking. As we talked, I realised that a number of them were committed Catholics. I wondered inwardly how this shaped their role as military generals – and the thought formed that perhaps this religious commitment might shape their ethics and attitude to war. So I took a bold plunge. I quoted from memory the words of Jesus from his Sermon on the Mount where he said, 'But I say to you who listen: Love your enemies, do what is good to those who hate you, bless those who curse you, pray for those who mistreat you. If anyone hits you on the cheek, offer the other also.'

I said that was the highest ethical standard and the most counterintuitive and radical teaching humankind has ever received. Most of us find it hard to tolerate our enemies, let alone contemplate loving our enemies. That is a bridge too far – when, for most of us, the first instinct is to just want to hit our enemies. So, heart in mouth, I asked how they, both as men of faith and military leaders, handled this teaching from the Sermon on the Mount.

A most engaged and robust debate broke out. As intelligent men, they took the question very seriously and wrestled with its implications. After some time, they had run down every possible implication and come to a consensus. For them, as military men and as Christians, they believed Jesus was teaching them to kill their enemies cleanly. Somewhat agog at this conclusion, I said I was pretty certain when he said 'love your enemies' he did not have that in mind!

The context of what we do and where we sit radically determines how we see life and how we interpret our faith. I am one who believes that war has outlived its usefulness as a tool for solving problems today. Whatever we once thought it achieved, it is clear that the damage and far-reaching consequences are not worth it. I think Jesus's way is a better path, and worth a try. Nations like Costa Rica have abolished their defence forces. In a lateral move, they have said they do not see any attack scenario realistic enough to justify spending such a huge percentage of their national budget on military costs. The enormous saving is going towards health and education, things that give their poor hope.

But I confess that if I was in the military, I might be thinking of Jack Nicholson's character in *A Few Good Men*. He contended that, as a citizen or non-combatant, you cannot handle the truth; you do not want to know what it takes to defend a nation. Maybe I can only sleep easy in my bed at night because the military is manning the barricades, prepared to do the things that I regard as brutal on my behalf to preserve my freedom.

I had a glimpse of that military culture on another occasion many years ago. I was the guest speaker for an officers' mess dinner on an army base. We had pre-dinner drinks and Peter Cosgrove, at the time the head of the defence forces, said, 'Tim, soon you will hear the one-minute whistle – and you will need to go the toilet before we go inside for dinner.'

I was a bit embarrassed and said, 'Thanks, but I am fine.'

He was insistent and said, 'No, let me explain. Once inside, there will be a four-hour dinner, with four different glasses at each place-setting – and if you have to get up and leave your seat to go to the toilet, then you may get humiliated.'

Needless to say I took his advice on the one-minute whistle.

There was great camaraderie that night, along with a lot of drinking. The thing that struck me most was members from different corps, like engineers or infantry, standing up in turn and singing their corps ditty. The words were banal and worse than football lyrics – 'we are bastards we are, we are the biggest bastards on earth' – but as they sang them, many of the men in the group had tears rolling down their faces. It was moving and scary to realise that for them, life and death depended on their loyalty and bonding to each other. It was all expressed in the ditty.

Football is preferable to war

At fifty-seven, I still play Australian Rules football in a competition for over-forty-sevens. We play a match every two weeks, because it takes us two weeks to recover. After a game, I can barely walk up the stairs to take a bath. Merridie thinks playing at my age is crazy and just part of an extended midlife crisis – and I tell her it's cheaper than a red sports car. As a contact sport, it is foolish at my age. But I love the physical contact and release of aggression. Guys with tattoos, no teeth and chequered histories make up the team. Our captain and best player's nickname is Mongo. When I asked him where that name came from, he told me he'd had it since primary school. I looked puzzled, and he explained: his surname is Lloyd, so they called him Mongo-Lloyd. Cruel, I know, but such names stick. I am called the Rev! In fact, none of us actually knows each other's real names, but that is no barrier to solidarity.

I run and get fit because I have a goal: to get through a game. I could never just train for its own sake. I have heard that people who jog every day live on average seven years longer than those who don't. The only problem is that they have spent those seven years jogging! But to be part of a team and not let them down is an incentive for me to jog.

Some believe that Australians' fascination and obsession with football is an echo of war. Young men with mud-splattered bodies, showing physical aggression in warring teams, reminds us of our nation's heroes, who showed such courage and sacrifice in war's trenches. For me, and for my sons who play in a local team, it seems to be a game that simply organises and channels our aggression. There are rules and an enemy to be beaten by kicking more goals and, best of all, there is a sense of remarkable belonging. Guys support each other and share in ways that are different from women. When a woman says to her girlfriends, 'Let's have a coffee', they know exactly what they are going to do. An hour later, they have workshopped their feelings and emotions. Relationships and processing important things is permissible and obvious. Many men have a coffee and drink it in five minutes and say goodbye because they have finished the coffee! Football, sporting teams and physical challenge give men a leave pass. After a football game, there is a release of tension and permission to talk about off-limits issues – because we have struggled together.

It is certainly a much better outlet than war, with its appeal to aggressiveness and defeat of an enemy. What if international disputes were settled with a football game? A range of needs might be settled with a contest of national honour that did not wreak havoc and death. What are Olympic achievements about, if not in part a demonstration of national competitiveness.

Marriage milestones

Some years ago, my wife, Merridie, and I saw a play in London's West End. (We are opportunistic when it comes to a HalfTix window.) When I have a night off and the opportunity arises, we go for whatever play is on offer at the best price. This night it was not *Les Miserables* or *The Blue Room* but a play called *The Goat, or Who is Sylvia?*. It was close to our twenty-fifth wedding anniversary and 'The Goat' as a title seemed passing curious for a memorable night.

It was indeed curious, as it turned out. The play was about a couple where the wife became increasingly convinced her husband was having an affair. All the tell-tale signs of a man in love – that a wife can easily sense – were there. As the play unfolded, she was proved to be right. He was having an affair. The twist was that he was in love – with a goat.

We were treated to his love poetry and soaring transformation when he looked into the eyes of the goat. It was a true love story with intense feelings and sublime lostness in love. He had discovered in falling in love with the goat a part of himself that was being set free. The range of his emotional response left you thinking, 'Well why not? He is clearly not crazy, so who are we to judge?' He was so insightful and honest as he confided to a friend what a better man, a man with deeper convictions, he had become. But, carried as we were by the passion and authenticity of his human experience, there was the jarring reminder – it's still a goat.

Of course, that was the point. When his wife discovers who it is, she kills the goat. The play ends with her dragging a dead goat on to the stage and the curtain falls with him sobbing inconsolably, cradling in his lap the head of the slain goat. Shocked with this ending, you cannot help feeling furious at this jealous, murderous, unforgiving wife. Then caught up in the moment of sympathy for his pain and loss, you think: but … it was a goat.

Falling in love is the most sublime human experience. What is an affair then? Maybe it's more of the same. Or maybe the other person has become the vehicle for release from a limited and nailed-down identity. It is about me – about what is lacking in my own self, the work I have not faced up to doing. About the known self that effortlessly jumps out of a small box, as marriage might feel at times, and becomes different, freely able to cross boundaries. It is the crossing of these former boundaries and the sense of freedom that comes from this new connection with another that is sublime. But this same freedom and crossing of boundaries falls foul of religious and cultural taboos. Loyalty and commitments dissolve because this new love has to be pursued at all costs to reach this new self – or to find a fresh sense of happiness.

I refuse to be quick to judge anyone who has an affair or whose marriage breaks down. None of us can truly know another's marriage, so we cannot claim to understand the full story. But the goat is a cautionary reminder that behaviour may be triggered by primary forces that come from dissatisfaction with the self – not the perfection and idealisation of the new love in contrast with the old commitment and the years of 'ordinary' life that have been built together.

To remain married across many years and for it to be a relationship in which one is fulfilled and content requires a good deal of self-discovery. It is a journey well worth the effort. To know oneself and to be truly known is what gives love its best chances of longevity.

* * *

Shortly after seeing *The Goat, or Who is Sylvia?* Merridie and I flew home to Melbourne together. She had only been with me for six days – the first time she had flown alone and met me on the international trips that were becoming part and parcel of my work. Her days had been full of sightseeing around London – a city both of us love.

We boarded a Qantas flight at 11 pm and Merridie sat up against the window in our row of three in economy. I was in the middle and, for the first leg, an American who was only slightly smaller than Texas was on the aisle seat. Needless to say, we were packed in.

For the next twelve hours or so to Singapore, both of us slept extensively – Merridie barely moved. I knew she was totally exhausted.

Arriving in Singapore after such a long flight is disorienting at the best of times. This time I noticed that Merridie seemed to be breathing heavily and found it hard to walk for long in the huge airport. She felt annoyed that she must have picked up a cold in the aircraft cabin and simply wanted to lie down and sleep anywhere she could find.

So we boarded again and prepared ourselves for an early Sunday morning arrival in Melbourne. Once we got home from the airport, Merridie showered and told me that she felt she was going to faint and was not at all well. Her breathing remained laboured. Finally, after an hour or two on the couch where she felt no better, we decided to go to a local twenty-four-hour medical clinic for her to be checked. Both of us suspected sudden-onset pneumonia. It took no time for the Indian-born doctor to think otherwise. She instructed us to go immediately to the emergency department at our closest public hospital.

The treatment Merridie received – being immediately given a bed in our notoriously busy emergency ward and being put on oxygen – made me realise something serious was happening. Or had happened. Various scans showed her lungs were full of minuscule clots. A deep vein thrombosis had gone through her heart to her lungs. She had pulmonary embolism and was lucky to be alive.

I went home and gathered our three children – all living at home at that time – and we went back to see her. By then the news was a little clearer. Her body had been checked and no further clots were found; her blood was now being thinned and she looked a better colour. Merridie, the one we all depended on, was going to be okay.

For me the whole experience happened in a jet-lagged blur, but I do remember the terrible realisation of how close I came to having Merridie die beside me on that flight. I know it could have happened in seconds – a clot can travel to the brain or can block blood from the heart. Our twenty-five years together could have ended in one rogue moment.

I knew then and know now that nothing else matters as much as life. It is when it is threatened or in some cases taken that we realise how much the essence of another person means to us.

* * *

Five years later, Merridie again flew to meet me on the other side of the world. This time I took two weeks of annual leave – a thirty-year anniversary deserves it!

We had one week to explore Ireland in a hired car. We decided to explore my family roots – my great-great-grandfather having left during the potato famine in 1842. We even found a Costello Chapel in the main street of Carrick-on-Shannon in County Leitrim – the smallest Catholic chapel in Europe. In fact, it is a crypt that Edward Costello built for his wife, Mary Josephine, who predeceased him prematurely. He was so besotted by her that he built this memorial chapel where masses were held each month for the remainder of his lifetime.

This being Ireland, the storekeeper told us we must have a cup of tea with Mary Costello, as she knew everyone's story. She pointed out Mary's home. We knocked on Mary's door and without hesitation she invited us in – even though we were total strangers with the flimsiest of links: a shared surname. Mary proceeded to lavish us with fresh scones and tea. Neither of us had any idea if there was a family connection, as the Irish records pre-1830 were destroyed in the fighting and burning of the 1916 Easter uprising. But Irish graciousness and the love of family and a good story overwhelmed those quibbling details. I felt like I belonged with this tribe in some way or another.

We drove on to Clifden, a town close to Croagh Patrick, the mountain Saint Patrick is believed to have climbed, and checked into a cute bed and breakfast in the main street. After a meal and a walk we retired, only to be awoken a few hours later by a domestic dispute. The noise was coming from the room above us and we quickly realised the row was between the proprietors. She was screaming at him.

'For t'irty years, *t'irty* years I have stayed with you, cleaned and cooked and raised your children. And it has been *t'irty* years of misery and hell!' We couldn't hear his quiet response.

I rolled over and said to Merridie, '*T'irty years.*' I did hear her response: 'Yep, know the feeling!' Fortunately, we both laughed.

We were not to know the reason for the outburst, but the next morning they were a picture of partnership, with her cooking and him serving us a big hearty breakfast with a smile and Irish charm. Maybe that is one secret of marital longevity. Let the toxins out in private, but then it's on with getting the work done in the morning.

Our second week saw us in Paris. If I had realised how quickly this city allows a man to get out of the debit side of the ledger and into credit in his relationship, I would have played the Paris card much earlier.

We soaked up the city of love, enjoying its history, cafes and street life. One day we sat in Cafe de Flore imagining ourselves into the lives of Jean Paul Sartre and Simone de Beauvoir. Another day we took the brilliant historic walk that takes in the revolutionary sites and stories around the Latin Quarter. On our last full day we found ourselves waiting in a queue at the Musée D'Orsay. A couple in front, upon hearing us talking, wheeled around and asked if we were Aussies. With our nods he said, 'I am Bob and this is my wife, Sheila. We're from Port Macquarie. I'm a plumber. So what do you do, mate?'

I said, 'I work for a charity in Australia.'

'Great,' he said, 'which one?'

'World Vision,' I replied.

'Oh yeah, that's great; so would you know Tim Costello?'

Quick as a flash Merridie intervened and said 'Yes, but not very well.'

Sheila got it instantly, nervously laughed and nudged Bob – filling him in, as only wives can do.

How well did I know myself? The person closest to you always is the best judge of the blind spots.

We discovered that the day before they had 'done' the Louvre Museum in an hour because they got bored so I encouraged them to take my advice and do a guided tour with us. At that point Bob and Sheila wanted their picture taken with me. I saw the look Merridie flashed me after she handed them back their camera.

To know yourself is to listen to criticism from others, however confronting. Perhaps especially from the ones who know us best. Why do I find myself saying yes so often to the requests of others, which means often denying my wife and family for strangers? Is it a need to be needed? Is it guilt because I think that it is what Christian faith demands of me?

My wife is right. I am sure I do not know Tim Costello very well.

Redemption and lifesaving

Where we holiday at the beach each year, we walk the rugged cliffs most evenings to absorb the horizons. We see ships heading to Asia, New Zealand and South America. They are just specks on the horizon in the vast ocean. It makes me feel insignificant. But my faith says that the Creator of the many universes cares for me. How do I hold this together with the smallness of my life and the awesome notion of galaxies spinning in space and billions of years of life on earth?

I remember sitting in the gutter beside a heroin addict years ago, when I worked for a city-based charity. I was trying to convince him to go into a drug rehabilitation program that we were connected to. He had been attending the Credo Cafe street lunches that Urban Seed runs for the homeless.

I remember saying something that came incredibly easily to me. It rolled off my tongue almost unconsciously. 'You know I believe that God made you.' That simple statement opened up a well of tears in the man. I wondered what I had said and done. Then, through the tears, he blurted out, 'God made me? But me old man told me I was just an accident.'

My words had touched a nerve. Out rolled a story of only being a burden, an interruption – a waste of space. So the story I had given him was a completely novel notion. I could see him trying to process a radical idea that turned his self-belief on its head – God somehow made me.

It was the leverage I needed to help him find motivation to get clean and then do some real work to discover his potential and reason for being here. This is redemption. A being found, a reclaiming of the deeper purpose for which we are here. Another example of how the stories we tell to children can determine so much.

At our wider family's beach house are many books. In fact, it probably has the most eclectic collection possible. I hate getting rid of anything, but Merridie likes to regularly de-clutter. I will often drop in at the local surf lifesaving club opportunity shop to peruse the bookshelves, and I have even found myself inadvertently re-buying books she had given them freely. The women managing the shop recognise me, smile knowingly and offer to give them back. But I insist on paying for what I once owned. They shake their heads, accepting the donation to the lifesaving cause and laugh at our marriage – particularly when the last one I re-bought was called *The Restored Relationship*!

It illustrates my practical view of redemption. It was always mine and was wrongly lost or unlawfully disposed of and so I have willingly, evenly joyfully, paid again for what was originally mine. To my heroin-addicted friend I explained that he was made by God and lost to a lesser story that told him he was just a waste of space. Redemption is about being brought back into a true lifesaving story. A story that tells him he is here for a reason and can be all that his potential allows and not be robbed of it by addiction. He can belong again to the one who created him for deeper purposes.

The Eruv

Merridie and I live in the Eruv. Not by plan, nor deliberate choice. We only discovered this after we had been living there ten years. 'Eruv' is a Yiddish word that describes a concept based on the walls of Jerusalem. Outside was unclean and inside was the presence of God in the holy city. In our case, it means the Jewish part of Melbourne. Delineated by Orthodox rabbis, who indicated the outer boundaries with marked lampposts, the Eruv means all the streets within can be regarded as private, just like your own home. Practically, it means you can leave your home on the Sabbath (Saturday) and have a stroll without breaking the Jewish law. You are technically still in your own home, resting on the Sabbath. Neat. Upon discovering this, we felt we were among the chosen – on sacred ground and with a leave pass to enjoy a special freedom within the walls of the law.

Of course, it was a fleeting joy, because as Gentiles it hardly matters to us – much as we notice it doesn't matter to so many secular Jews who also live alongside us in the Eruv. Maybe our joy was more to do with the hope that we have a slightly enhanced house price for Eruv-seeking buyers! It made me wonder about the law and holiness. I had been requested on a few occasions to come into Jewish homes or businesses after sundown on Friday to flick a switch or change a light bulb that had blown on the Sabbath. The person making the request would not sin but, I wondered as I twisted the dead light bulb out and replaced it with a new one, why was it okay in their eyes for *me* to sin? If it is God's law, why should it not be universal and also wrong for me? Is the law only for Jewish believers? Now, many Jewish homes are fitted with timers that trigger all internal lights and ovens after sundown to avoid breaching the Sabbath. Flats and apartment complexes have lifts running continuously to avoid the transgression of pushing the button. And the technical fix of 'being in your home' when you are actually out in public on the street seems a bit too orchestrated.

But the bookends of faithfulness to religious authority and contemporary relevance are not just a Jewish challenge. I grew up in a mental Eruv. I remember my brother and I feeling so guilty when we secretly snuck away from home for the first time to watch our football team play on a Sunday in 1984. Sunday was our 'Sabbath', or day of rest, and watching football was unacceptable then.

Indeed, I felt in our Eruv that we belonged to a secret tribe with its own special language called the language of Christian Zion. We had our Christian music, heroes and even definition of fun, as we were saved and the rest were not. So we were to be a witness in a hostile, godless world, and be an example of holiness that would attract others to faith. Mostly the others seemed confused by our rules and culture of not dancing, drinking or smoking. It appeared to others that if it was pleasurable, then we must define it as wrong. But somehow for us it made sense. At the time we did not question why it was okay to watch *World of Sport* on TV in our own homes on a Sunday, but not to go to a game. We knew somehow that would be a bad witness to 'outsiders'.

* * *

I gradually came to understand that all of life is sacred. That God did not just belong to Christians or, as Archbishop Tutu puts it in the title of one of his books, 'God is not a Christian'. That is a big jump from a sectarian background, and a painful journey from believing 'I have the big secret and it belongs to my tribe and its truth can only be expressed in my biblical language of Zion'.

The walls of the Eruv encompass not just my mob, but extend to the four winds. As the old spiritual put it, 'He's got the whole world in his hands'. My faith is still constantly stretched. I don't have answers to the death of children, or the onset of cruel mental illness. There are times when all I can do is to sit in silence before the face of suffering and hope that with time and kindness the worst of the grief will pass. There are few instant miracle cures. And meeting people of other faiths or being challenged by people's dedication and belief always opens me to seeing my own faith in fresh ways.

In 2005 I visited north-west Pakistan, where World Vision was responding in many villages after a fearsome earthquake had killed 80,000 people. This was an area where there were many fundamentalist Muslims – where Osama bin Laden reputedly did some successful recruiting. As I sat with the bearded men in robes and turbans, one of them said to me, 'Why is World Vision, a Christian humanitarian organisation, helping us in our suffering?' He was so thankful we were helping but also so surprised. I heard myself say, 'Because Jesus did not say, "Just love Christians". We are all God's children.' Even as I said these words, I found myself in an out-of-body moment, surprised at observing how far I had come in my journey.

Within this global Eruv, we are all under one law and one Creator. The law of love. Put in my language, it means that everyone is made in the image of God and of equal worth. Put in the language of secular human rights, it says that human rights are universal and indivisible because injustice to anyone, anywhere is an injustice done to me. Same effect, just different expressions. No man is an island. We are interconnected and family. The walls of language and culture that mark us off in each other's minds as so utterly different and scary are only skin deep.

Recently I went to the Melbourne Zoo for an event. While there, I was informed by a specialist staff researcher that we now know that a bunch of forty apes, which have been interbreeding with each other in the Melbourne Zoo for the last twenty years, have more genetic diversity among them than the whole human race. Racism is truly revealed to be nonsense with the DNA code cracked. Nationalism is a construct imposed for control. While belief systems do matter, it is humbling to recall that they are culturally shaped. I know that if I was born in Iran, there is a 90 per cent chance that I would be a Shi'a Muslim, not a Baptist. We are one global family, and that should characterise how we treat and respect each other.

Family is the great driving force of history. Think how parents will make unbelievable personal sacrifices just so their children can have a better life than they did. To their own disadvantage, sacrificing health and enduring long work hours, they willingly make these sacrifices. My parents did, as theirs before them did. If we are all family, the children of the world, wherever they live, deserve our generosity and sacrifices so they can have a better future.

That is a world vision for a global Eruv. It shapes my ethics today. I rarely hesitate to throw a few coins to a fellow Australian who is on the street with a sign saying 'hungry and homeless'. If I think that they will just drink it, I call an outreach worker. Why? Because I feel an ethical tug: this is a fellow Australian. I cannot walk on by. So if I believe all people are part of my family, made in the image of God, and that they should enjoy universal rights, free from hunger and homelessness, then there should be an ethical tug wherever they live, whatever their colour and creed. Those are the ethics for a global Eruv.

The final picture of heaven in the New Testament is all nations, cultures and language groups of the world streaming together to the New Jerusalem. What is striking is that Jerusalem is now pictured as a city without walls. There is no need as there are now no enemies and there is no culture outside where it is profane or unclean. The global eruv has come on earth.

Fear never leaves us

After the Holocaust, many survivors took out a map and asked themselves where the furthest place from the horrors they had suffered would be. Many settled on Australia, the opposite side of the globe to Europe and its death camps. Melbourne already had a large Jewish community from before the war. Now we have one of the largest Holocaust-survivor communities anywhere in the world. This is the area of Melbourne where Merridie and I have lived for the last twelve years.

One of our good friend's parents both survived Auschwitz. Her mother, who is still alive, has some of the attendant issues that terrible memories compounded with old age and ill health create. When we talk about the future for the state of Israel, I can talk easily and theoretically. Having travelled to Israel many times, I find it easy to ask Jews who I talk to: why should Melbourne or New York Jews, who have never had any family ties with Israel, benefit from the Law of Return that gives them a second home outside Australia or the US in the Palestinian-occupied territories? Why should they be able to displace Palestinians, who have been there for centuries, from their homes? Another question that bothers me is: why does Israel need the bomb, but deny other nations the same?

But these are theoretical questions. My family did not die in the Holocaust. I do not have relatives who have survived and can never forget. The answer is rooted in a primal fear. Who predicted the sudden morphing of centuries of European anti-Semitism into the Holocaust? My Jewish friends believe such an unanticipated wave of irrational prejudice can arise suddenly without warning again, anywhere and at any time. And without a Jewish state with the bomb for defence, where would they flee next time for safety?

I have spoken at a number of synagogues and been honoured by the Jewish community. I was the third Gentile in Australian history to be awarded the Raoul Wallenberg award for Righteous Gentile by B'nai B'rith – the Jewish human rights society. It is one of my proudest honours. But I am also a patron for Palestinian Christians who want their occupied lands and homes returned. Unlike Newt Gingrich, I do not believe Palestinians are an invented people.

Of course, we associate anti-Semitism with Arab nations today. But it was Christians in Europe who fanned anti-Semitism into murderous genocide. Europeans, including Christians like the Protestant reformer Martin Luther, not Palestinians, nurtured this evil. But presently it is Palestinians paying the price for their attitudes. I do not understand the power of Christian Zionism in evangelical churches, particularly in the US. And I wonder why the same people ignore the plight of Christian Palestinians.

I do think, however, that American Christian Zionism has been a bulwark against the Christian anti-Semitism that was so dominant in the churches of Europe in the nineteenth and twentieth centuries. Of course, there are ironies. The State of Israel no doubt appreciates the defence and foreign policy support that Christian Zionists afford in the US. It will rarely admit it, but equally it is not very comfortable with the theology behind Christian Zionism that insists on protecting a Jewish state and with the eventual location of Jerusalem as a solely Jewish capital. That theology is so militantly pro-Israeli because this is their interpretation of the Bible's prophetic pre-requisite for the return of Jesus. It will necessitate the conversion of Jews into Christians. That view of conversion is exactly where many European Christian anti-Semites started!

It is a hideously complicated scenario. Religion and politics converging at their complex best.

* * *

So where is the hope? Typically, you have to look beyond governments to people, who act with much greater courage and clarity. I sat in a World Vision–supported project one evening in Jerusalem and met some of these courageous people. It was one of the most moving nights of my life. Here were Israeli Jews and Israeli Arabs sitting together and talking. They formed what they called 'The Circle of the Bereaved'. They were all parents united by a common grief and showing remarkable courage to sit and listen to each other.

Their common grief was that they had lost children in the conflict. Each sat and listened to the painful stories from the other side of the divide, bonding with a common humanity that transcended ideology and politics. The Arab parents had lost sons and daughters who were killed by the Israeli Defence Forces (IDF). The Jewish parents had lost children to Shaheed, the Palestinian suicide bombers, or to rockets coming out of Gaza. Each told the concrete details of their loss, without recrimination but with explicit details. The most heart-wrenching experience of grief for both sides was being heard and validated. Grief observed unites.

I found myself often in tears through the night, as the accounts of young lives slaughtered were almost too much to bear. Telling the story of loss is in itself therapeutic and healing. But telling the story to the 'enemy' and receiving a sympathetic ear is altogether unprecedented. Some of the Arab children were just in the wrong place when an IDF operation was executed. Sometimes all it was for was to just send a message. And there they were – innocent bystanders. Many of the Jewish kids were killed without warning or any chance of escape. Sitting in a cafe or on a bus with their friends – maybe dreaming, as young people should do, of their futures. All shattered in one blinding moment when the human bomb was detonated.

As parents, we all want to die before our children. It is explosive to our sense of destiny to reverse the natural order. Rage and disbelief follows. What touched me was the extraordinary reaching out in compassion by people who had every reason to deeply hate each other and to seek revenge. They did not agree on political solutions or the complex history of and responsibility for the conflict. But one thing they all agreed on was that the killing must stop. Fear of each other must be dispelled, and that is best done face-to-face, with patient listening.

One Jewish parent heard about the circle after using a toll-free chat line set up by a charity so that Jews could talk to Arabs and Palestinians, thereby cutting through prejudice and propaganda. I will not forget her saying, 'My government does not want us to talk to each other, but to hate. But I had to get to know these people I hated and see their faces. Now I understand they have the same hopes and feelings as me. They are not terrorists.'

As Archbishop Tutu said, 'Without forgiveness there is no future.' Likewise, without searching to understand, there is no progress towards peace. Are we not all just frail humans trying to get by? I left the circle convinced that all political leaders in this complex situation needed to spend an evening sitting in this circle of the bereaved. Let them first listen, and then look into the eyes of grieving parents, and only then seek to justify proposed military actions to this group from both sides, before escalating the hostilities.

Still not a pretty story

One of the foundational stories of my childhood was the exodus of the Hebrew slaves from the enslavement of the pharaoh in Egypt. Today's Jewish community celebrates it every year with a Passover meal, so called because the angel of death passed over the homes of Jewish families, striking death to the first-born son in every Egyptian family.

In the story, this tenth curse was the big one after plagues of frogs and boils and rivers turning to blood had failed to persuade the pharaoh. The wailing of Egyptian mothers over the deaths of their eldest sons forced the reluctant pharaoh to finally let the children of Israel go. I have sat as a guest at several Passover meals in Jewish homes and eaten the flat bread and bitter herbs and listened to the story read solemnly by a rabbi.

It is not a pretty story but, like the American civil war, it is one of salvation for slaves. It took a civil war and 600,000 dead to end slavery in the US because it was just so profitable. And how the Israelites became slaves is still a pretty accurate picture for today's global economics and politics. There was a great administrator running the pharaoh's economy, called Joseph. He was put in charge, even though he was Hebrew, after interpreting the pharaoh's dream where he saw seven fat cows devouring seven thin cows. He had interpreted correctly that there would be seven years of economic boom followed by seven years of harvests failing and famine. His was an administration built on discipline and good governance. He built storehouses and squirrelled away grain and wheat and state assets, rather than seek public popularity by allowing the Egyptians conspicuous consumption and spending up big in the seven good years. Contrary to today's leaders in Europe and the US, who wasted the good years and kept on borrowing, Joseph was ready when the bad years hit. Instead of a debt blowout in good times, he was blessed with huge surpluses.

Then there was a great drought over the known earth that lasted seven years. In the first year, people from other nations, including Israelites, streamed into Egypt and handed over cash for grain and wheat. They thought that would tide them over until the drought broke. But then the famine continued in the second year and, having handed over all their cash the previous year, the Israelites came back and handed over their cattle (their only means of livelihood) for grain from Joseph's storehouses. But then the famine continued the next year, and back they came without cash or livestock, and said, 'We have nothing but ourselves to hand over. Better that we are slaves to the pharaoh and survive than see our children die of famine and drought.'

This is a familiar pattern today, only that the storehouses are in China when the US and other

Western nations go begging and borrowing to finance their debt. Debt is certainly the reason for much modern-day slavery. Few realise that there are today more slaves than ever before in history – some 21 million. That is more than during the whole 450 years of the Atlantic slave trade. Like the children of Israel, the current slaves are driven by crop failure, hunger and poverty. I have met mothers who have said through tears, 'I sold this child in the hope that with the money I would be able to feed the others.' Without addressing poverty, it is impossible to deal with modern-day slavery.

The Exodus story lives on today. There are children who are third-generation slaves in mills in India. It started with their grandfather, who had been forced to borrow from the moneylender when his crop failed. He thought he was repaying the loan, but was surprised to find he owed double the original debt because he had signed up to a small-print rate of 15 per cent weekly compound interest. In desperation to keep his farm and feed his other kids, he handed over his son to work as a bonded slave in the moneylender's mill. Soon that son had married, and still the debt was not paid – and so *his* son at twelve was handed over to work on the same site as a bonded slave. Their whole lives consumed because of a crop failure generations ago. In India, despite laws outlawing bonded child labour, an estimated 12 million children are enslaved today.

* * *

In 2007 I travelled to Ghana and to the Ivory Coast. Chocolate made me go. I had become disturbed by reports of kids being trafficked to work on the cocoa plantations. Chocolate is one of life's pleasures, but most of us have a guilt relationship with chocolate. I am struck with how religious the language used to describe our relationship with chocolate is. Too much of it is a sin, and people need to go on fasts to deal with its temptation.

Some 70 per cent of the world's cocoa comes out of Ghana and the Ivory Coast. Cocoa trees need jungle and shade, and they need humidity for the cocoa pods to ripen on the trees. So the plantations are often in jungle villages, remote and in the bush, with terrible roads and few schools or health clinics. Yet this is where the guilty pleasure starts, with few prying eyes or questions from the consumer. In the Ivory Coast, the police in the capital showed us some pictures of traffickers they had arrested crossing with kids from poor bordering nations. Of course, these kids did not get paid, nor did they get to go to school or have any rights. They were slave labour. Now that it was known and some outside pressure was being applied, the traffickers had become more sophisticated. We saw pictures of buses disguised as ambulances with the kids dressed in bandages to fool anyone who asked. The policeman showing us the pictures admitted that with only one police car at his disposal, the stemming of this tide was futile.

We journeyed on the bad roads out to the villages and saw kids harvesting the pods from the trees using razor-sharp machetes. We saw children spraying dangerous chemicals to kill off the weeds on the farms. So many of them appeared ill-fed and thin. We were told that many were far from home. Why? Because the economics determine that we in the West want to eat cheap chocolate. Suddenly I realised the sin was less about my guilty pleasure that put excess kilograms on my waistline. If I was to feel guilty, I now knew the real reason. It was a sin against children in the name of greater and cheaper production. Nor could I atone for this guilt by hitting the gym. I needed to speak up.

In Ghana we visited an old slave port on the way down to the cocoa farms. In the fort was a 'Door of No Return', because slaves who went through it to board the ship either died or, if they survived, never saw their families or homes again. And I thought slavery had been abolished.

Certainly, thanks to men like William Wilberforce, the right of humans to produce a certificate of title verifying they owned another human was abolished. But I was on my way to see the modern form of slavery. Many kids on these farms had entered through a door of no return to their families.

World Vision began a campaign called 'Don't trade lives', joining with other groups like 'Stop the Traffick'. We invited our supporters to send coupons to chocolate manufacturers and supermarkets saying we were prepared to pay an extra 10 cents for a block, knowing this could ensure proper wages for farmers and obviate the need for trafficked and exploited kids. Could they change to Fair

Trade and certify this? We explained why a modern slave trade was so profitable and that it was the third biggest commercial trade after armaments and drugs.

To some extent we were just picking up the successful first-ever public campaign led by Wilberforce in the early 1800s in the Parliament of Great Britain. He called for a boycott of sugar and tea in Britain, as it came from the sweat of slaves. His imagery was graphic. He appealed, 'When you put that sugar in your tea you do not want to have blood on your teeth.'

But unlike Wilberforce, we were not urging a boycott that could just throw desperately poor cocoa farmers out of work and occasion greater pain for children.

It worked. First Cadbury declared that its biggest selling Dairy Milk block would be Fair Trade by Easter 2010 – and they kept their word. Mars followed, as did Arnotts, the makers of the iconic Aussie chocolate biscuit the Tim Tam. But not all were as accommodating. For eighteen months I was dogged by the chocolate manufacturer's lobby, following me to speaking engagements and defending the industry. But there is nothing like having visited the farms and seeing for myself to cut through the arguments. This counted when I personally visited the chocolate-industry CEOs.

Look for the Fair Trade logo or a similar one from the Rainbow Alliance. Remember: the consumer, who has awakened their conscience to the real sin, rules.

Salvation that is public and personal

One of the stories I heard growing up was about a father who brought home a 1500-piece jigsaw puzzle of the world and gave it to his son. The father thought the puzzle would keep the boy occupied for a few weeks and give him some peace. His son tore into the challenge and, a few hours later, the father was amazed to hear his son shout from his bedroom, 'Dad, I've finished it.' In disbelief, he walked into his room and there was an exquisite and complex globe, all in perfect order. With pride he thought, This boy is so talented – finishing such a thing in record time. His son smiled and said, 'Dad, you don't realise something. You gave me a double-sided jigsaw puzzle. On one side was the world and that would have taken me weeks to assemble. But the picture on the other side was just a man. That side was dead simple so I started there. Once I had got the man right, I just had to turn the whole puzzle over and instantly the world was right.'

This story summed up the hope and theology of my early years. If 'the man', or people, could be saved and their hearts were right, the world would be right. We did not need to be diverted into struggling for social justice or challenging power structures – we just needed more people saved and the injustice would evaporate as their lives would then be right and they would live justly. It was all about the individual and their salvation.

But it was at university in 1977 that I discovered salvation must also be public and challenge society. My simple-sided jigsaw puzzle hopes fell apart when a South African preacher spoke to our university Christian society. He shocked me and other students when he said that his nation, structured as it was in 1977 by repressive apartheid, could blame church-attending, bible-believing Christians, as these were largely the people who had devised the system and supported its maintenance.

As a law student, I followed the story of the brutal death of black activist Steve Biko at the hands of the South African police. I was outraged by apartheid and even today can still feel the tremors that went through my body when I first heard from this South African preacher that apartheid owed some of its inspiration and justification to prayerful church-attending Christians. So just getting people saved was not enough – and, worse, it might even result in them legislating entrenched racial injustice.

Now there was a much deeper challenge. I could argue that these South Africans were not true Christians but I knew that was a dead end. My personal view about salvation needed to change. I went back to study the teaching of Jesus and realised that his emphasis was on embracing the rule of God and how that rule looked out for the people with little or no power in society.

I understood for the first time that the hope of the Gospel must address the big issues of racism and power – otherwise, it was not the whole Gospel of Jesus. My understanding of salvation had to be deepened and broadened, or my faith had only limited relevance.

I still believe that people need a personal change of heart. My faith is personal. I believe that Jesus died for me. But I also see that salvation is public – that it addresses the power structures that dehumanise people. It is not just an individualistic experience but is also a means by which societies turn around and justice is brought to bear.

The jigsaw puzzle does have two sides, and each is part of the story. They work in tandem – we need the world to be saved or at least to hear the hope of how it might be rightly ordered before God as much as we need the individual person to find forgiveness and the experience of grace and salvation.

The most evil man in the world?

I was in London at World Vision meetings when a strange thing occurred. National directors started getting digital messages from their kids. 'Dad, do you know about this man? What is World Vision doing about him?' My son Martin was one of them. At the school where he taught, he had been overrun by kids who wanted to show him a YouTube video.

The 'Kony 2012' phenomenon had hit the world. Over 70 million people have viewed it. The organisation that created the video, Invisible Children, had a worldwide phenomenon on their hands. Kony, the fulcrum of all that is evil (as we were told), was on the radar – in the crosshairs of everyone with access to a computer.

As I did TV interviews from Westminster that night for Australia's breakfast talk shows, I wondered what note to strike. It was marvellous that such morally serious issues – child soldiers and the cruelty of Kony and the Lord's Resistance Army – were the world's talking point. People who never engaged with poverty issues were talking about it. But it was also a big simplification to talk about it as ridding the world of evil.

We'll 'get Kony' was the promise made by the filmmaker to his five-year-old son, Gavin. But what about the 21,000 kids who die every day of preventable diseases because their parents are poor? Where was the 'Get Poverty' video on YouTube? Poverty is what breeds a Kony. What about a 'Get Slavery' video to combat the 20 million people in slavery – most of them women and children – because our consumer supply chains depend on child labour? If we got Kony, what would change? If successful, maybe there would be hope for these other campaigns. But if it failed to find Kony, who in any event was a spent force and probably sitting under a banana tree in the Congolese jungle, maybe we would have the legacy of a generation of cynics who felt that global engagement did not work. That it was all a marketing ploy for wristbands and posters.

I remember visiting Gulu in Northern Uganda in 2006, at the height of the Kony-led kidnapping rampages. It was harrowing. At World Vision's war rehabilitation centre I watched former Kony slaves, who had either escaped or been left for dead, in rehabilitation. It was confronting to see them doing therapeutic street theatre with sticks for guns. They were acting out the horrors they had been through, attacking and kidnapping – bringing the past alive so that it could be finally put to rest.

I watched our centre's leader, Grace, inviting escapees to stand in a circle and throw the few possessions they had brought from the bush onto a fire. I watched their tears and anguish as they destroyed all remnants of their past. A past where they had been brainwashed to believe that the enemy's bullets would pass through them without injury if they were loyal to Kony. They then stood with linked arms and sang 'Amazing Grace'. That hymn has never felt more meaningful to me than when sung in that setting: 'I once was lost but now am found'.

I sat with a fourteen-year-old soldier who explained how, after being kidnapped by Kony, his first mission was to kill someone from his own clan – his uncle, a man he had loved and respected. If he refused, he would be tortured and killed by the others. Once he had killed his uncle, he belonged to Kony – he could never go back.

The most emotional moment was watching one young man who had finished his rehabilitation. He hugged the others and said goodbye, and then we travelled with him back to his village. He was seeing his family for his first time after two years in the LRA. It made me weep as we watched his mother fall on her knees, her arms open to him. He ran straight into her arms and they rolled together in the red dirt with shrieks of joy and consolation. The villagers gathered around to watch. Some welcomed him back – others looked wary and strained.

Every night at dusk, the roads into the main town of Gulu were packed with families and kids streaming in from all quarters. Thousands walked from their villages each evening to sleep in the night dormitories that were especially built to protect the people from the Kony raiders who always terrorised at night.

While Kony has been off the scene in Northern Uganda for many years, the work of reconciling families and communities, as well as mending young lives and hearts, will go on for years. As will the work to turn the entrenched poverty in that area around.

Yes I want them to 'get' Kony. He is evil. But I understand the anger of the Ugandans who threw stones at the screen when they watched 'Kony 2012' for the first time. They felt that the message, that some Americans had finally discovered Kony and now would save them, trivialised their pain.

We can celebrate the sentiment and idealism behind this campaign. But it is what the world, including the over 70 million people who have seen the clip, does to fix the underlying issues, the systemic poverty and slavery, that counts.

Who owns the sky?

In 2009 I attended the Copenhagen Climate Change Conference. I was there because of the work World Vision undertakes in many countries that stand to be gravely affected by the slightest rise in temperatures, volatile weather and rising sea levels. In particular, this included our work in low-lying islands in the Pacific. Like all other participants, I stood in queues for hours in the cold weather to attend each day. Freezing to the bone for the sake of global warming was a touch ironic!

The world's leaders gathered with high hopes that they could act collectively to overcome a common threat. Sadly, those hopes were dashed. What we saw was general agreement that the danger of a few degrees of warming was real if we did not curb putting carbon into the sky, but no binding agreement on who would make the cuts and slow their economic growth by pricing cheap and dirty fossil-fuel energy.

It became a question of who owned the sky and who had the right to put more carbon into the atmosphere for their national growth. The developing world's sentiments were that industrialised nations had been polluting with carbon for the last 200 years, a by-product of their industrial growth and enviable lifestyle. Now it was their turn to make deep cuts and give the developing nations a break – to let them grow and lift their people out of poverty. The West's response was that, with China and India becoming equal polluters to the US, they too had to make deep cuts or all would be doomed. They could not agree.

It reminded me of a birthday party I went to with one of my children. After 'Happy Birthday' was sung and the candles were blown out, the mother started cutting up the cake into equal pieces. An American mum asked what she was doing. She said, 'Well, we give each child a piece and the children can eat it here or take it home.'

The American mum said, 'But is that fair?'

Puzzled, the Australian said, 'Well, each kid gets a piece, and the same-sized piece, so what could be fairer?'

The response was fascinating. 'But you have not asked the kids. Some may not want any piece and some a smaller piece or larger. You have just decided for them.'

Both viewpoints are strands of justice. Equality and sameness, or choice and personal ownership. In development, we know that asking the community what they want and what effort they will make is fundamental to ownership. We must not impose our view of fairness on them in the interests of sameness.

At Copenhagen, the developing world was arguing equity given size. When an Indian carbon footprint is 1.6 tonnes per person, compared with 24 tonnes per person in the West, that is not fair and we should make cuts and let them grow with a bigger carbon emission. It is inequitable otherwise. They were saying, in effect,

'We own as much of the sky with our billions of people as you do in the West with far fewer.'

We were answering, 'But our people require this-size piece, and we cannot take it from them by curbing carbon and economic growth without them seeing you make an equal sacrifice. We in the West have a political challenge with constituencies who will not wear any cuts in lifestyle because they are used to a bigger piece.' The global consensus split on who owned the sky and which strand of justice resonated with them.

Of course, the hope is that we can do more with less by living within carbon limits and still see clean energy lead to economic growth. But it was hard to feel anything but quiet despair on the flight home. I know that fear and despair are not the answer. The complex issue of climate change must continue to be the focus of our best and brightest minds, so we can find ethical solutions to safeguard the future of the planet for all the world's children's children.

From a faith perspective, living with carbon constraint and scarcity, because this is all the sky we have, only makes sense if we can say with the Psalmist the earth (and the sky) is the Lord's. We do not own the right to do what we want without thought for others or the next generations. Those who have put the least carbon up there are the poorest nations. It is a matter of justice that it is precisely these nations, because they are poor, that are least protected from the worst impacts of a global warming in droughts, cyclones, floods and calamitous weather volatility.

The illicit money trail

During almost a decade as head of World Vision Australia, I have witnessed firsthand the suffering and devastation caused by some of the worst natural disasters. I have spoken to people who live in the poorest corners of the world and who daily fight simply to get enough food to survive.

My first shocking encounter with this poverty was speaking to a mother in the Philippines who could not afford both food for her children and medicine for one of the children who had fallen sick. She made the agonising decision to buy food and had to watch as her daughter died of disease.

I have also had the privilege of encountering communities that have defeated all the odds of poverty and disease to not only survive but thrive.

Yet when I consider the global fight against poverty, there is nothing more dispiriting, more sapping of enthusiasm and more lethal to hope than corruption. When we think of corruption, we often think of countries like Zimbabwe, Burma or Nigeria. We think of corrupt African rulers who steal from their people and channel illicit funds to secret offshore accounts. Indeed, there has been a tragic history of high-level kleptomania that has robbed the world's poorest nations.

In Australia and most western nations, you do not become rich by going into politics. Yet one of the reasons why you go into politics in many poor nations is precisely in order to become rich. But this is only possible on a grand scale with the use of offshore accounts.

It is important to recognise the wider context of these offshore accounts. They exist in offshore tax havens, which are shrouded in secrecy. There are sixty such 'secrecy jurisdictions' that have been created by Western countries such as Switzerland, the Netherlands, Britain (the City of London) and the US. Ironically, these are the countries that perform best on Transparency International's perception of corruption index.

This reflects how narrow our thinking about corruption has been. Capital flight out of African nations is well known. But the flight out has a corresponding flight in somewhere else. The bankers in the West provide safe havens for this capital and reap lucrative fees from their services. The simple fact is corrupt dictators cannot funnel out their stolen assets without banks and regulations in the first world that permit it and, of course, profit from it. It is estimated that for every $1 that is given in aid to poor nations, $10 flows out of these countries via secret jurisdictions through theft, the proceeds of crime and lost tax revenue.

It is a problem that goes beyond corrupt political leaders; it also involves major corporations avoiding tax that poor nations should be receiving. Developing countries lose an estimated $160 billion each year in tax revenue through corporate use of offshore jurisdictions. It is a stunning figure given that total foreign aid each year totals $120 billion. It has been estimated that this $160 billion could save the lives of 1,000 children under the age of five every day.

The supply and demand of this trade means we have to work on corruption at both ends, not just on the corrupt politicians in developing nations. This is not an issue that pits developed countries against developing nations. It is ultimately a story of how wealthy and powerful insiders make the rules for themselves through changing domestic tax systems and offshore activities. The result is that the rich and large corporations are not paying their fair share of tax and everyone else is left to pick up the tab.

The good news is that many non-government organisations are starting to make people aware of the insidious impact of these secret jurisdictions. They are starting to demand greater transparency from their governments; they are taking on the might of the financial lobby and seeking reforms that will favour developing countries that are being so adversely affected.

At the end of the day, governments and corporations will only be moved to act if people – voters, customers – demand it. The voices of the people are slowly starting to be heard, I am hopeful theirs will be a powerful call for change. Yet I am also very conscious that power and wealth is never surrendered without a struggle.

Don't email,
talk to me

I was listening to a panel where Jack Dorsey, the chair and creator of Twitter, was talking in Los Angeles a couple of years ago. He cautioned against thinking that you could build a movement through tweeting. It was a tool, like the telegram and the telephone, and it could no more get you off the couch and onto the streets than any other communication tool.

On the panel was the CEO of Invisible Children, a pioneer American charity. He backed Dorsey up by explaining how they had won the Chase Manhattan bank offer of $1 million to the charity that could show they had the most support for a project. When the challenge was announced, the email address lists of charities across the US went into overdrive. Charity protocol dictates that you do not send your supporters and donors more than two emails a week, as it annoys them. Invisible Children had pleaded for their base to email support for them and, in desperation at the meagre response, sent out a third email saying, in effect, 'we know you will be pissed off but isn't it worth being pissed off for one million dollars?' The response was still underwhelming, so they did something very countercultural for young people. They decided to phone and talk to their 70,000 supporters.

Given that text messaging is the way to communicate today, young people are genuinely surprised when the phone rings. Wow, who could that be? When asked about supporting Invisible Children, all said that yes, they had seen the emails and, of course, now that they had been rung and asked, they would respond (which took as little effort as pushing a send button). But it took a human voice to get action, not an electronic message. Invisible Children won the prize.

A human voice can communicate seriousness and sincerity just by the use of tone. It is the real medium for care and action. It cannot be easily dismissed.

I often wonder if next generations will experience the sensuality of holding a book of thoughtful letters, written with emotion and intention, as in the past. Who will collect bound volumes of emails dashed off with little thought (let alone the use of correct grammar)? The medium does not lend itself to sensitivity and feeling. There should be a rule in offices: you can send a certain number of emails per day to colleagues sitting a few desks away; once you hit that limit, you have to stretch your legs and look into their faces and actually talk to them.

Coping with Twitter has become a challenge. I think I am saying something very challenging and context-specific to the group in front of me and then find young people tweeting it around the world with no context. It scares me. I have learnt some simple rules. Do not tweet anything late at night, when you have had more than one drink or, particularly, when you think you are being funny. Sometimes the tweets are screened behind you as you are still giving your speech. Talk about an instant assessment. It feels like getting a film review and its rating before the film has finished.

Generation gaps are real

I remember, as a kid, sitting in the back of my father's FJ Holden as we pulled up at a service station. Back then we called them a garage. We three kids got out and watched my father lift the bonnet and fiddle around, checking the water and oil. We knew that was the limit of his mechanical skill, as he was a teacher and was just filling in time until the attendant came and filled up the tank. What struck me was that my father would always have a conversation with the attendant. He would crack a joke, ask about the football and even stray into politics. He taught politics at school, and the family was to become known for politics, with my brother Peter ending up as Federal Treasurer for eleven years. I was proud of Dad because he often did not know these attendants, and yet was so naturally able to find a point of connection and have a laugh. I remember the swelling feeling of pride at his ease with total strangers and thinking, 'I hope I can do that when I grow up.' That is how we all learn: through informal modelling.

Fast-forward many years later, and I had my three young kids in our Tarago van. Attendants now never leave the security counter, and so I filled up the tank, walked in and paid by credit card, signing and taking my receipt. As I roared off, I had the flashback to my father and thought, 'I did that transaction without even exchanging any words.' Efficient in time, yes – but what was I failing to model to my kids?

The next time I had my children with me was at a McDonald's, and I was ready to do better. The attendant had a name badge on, so in front of my kids I began: 'Hi Karen are you having a nice day?' She looked a little surprised and, mistaking this, I said, 'Oh sorry, I know your name but you don't know mine – my name is Tim.' Karen now looked a bit suspicious. I asked my kids to give their orders and, as she busied herself, I casually asked if this was a full-time or part-time job. She said full-time, so I asked if there was a career there and would she like to one day manage a McDonald's. She laughed and said, 'No, this is a job to pay the bills – I am a musician, and we are all poor.' I thought, 'This is good. This is a straight commercial transaction, but she has told me something of her dreams and hopes.' As we talked, I slowly turned to make sure my children were absorbing this modelling.

To my shock, they had all walked out and were nowhere to be seen. I placed the food on the table and rounded them up from on the street. No sooner had we sat down than my daughter rounded on me and said, 'Dad, you are such a nerd.'

I protested, 'What do you mean?'

She said, 'You are not meant to talk to her, and certainly not meant to call her by name.'

Feeling defensive, I said, 'If I am not meant to call her by name, why does she have a name badge on?'

My daughter explained as if I was really slow. 'She has a name badge so that if she stuffs up or keeps us waiting too long, we know who to report.' I was floored. We were both looking at the same thing – a name badge – but it had completely different meanings to us. I thought it was to assist friendliness and community. Not at all – my daughter explained it was all about accountability and customer service.

That is a generation gap. How often do we think we are talking about the same thing, but talking completely past each other? Although we speak the same language, now I pause to ask young people if they are seeing what I see, and what it means to them, rather than assume I know.

What does that sibling
of yours think of that?

Happy families are all alike but unhappy families are all unhappy in their own special way, according to Tolstoy. Most of us spend much of the rest of our lives working off the family script that was written in our childhood. I remember once being interviewed by a well-known broadcaster on ABC Radio National. After expressing my view on some issue, he feigned shock and said, 'And what does that sibling of yours think of that view?' I quietly responded that my sister totally agreed with me. He was now in overdrive.

'I've never heard of your sister – it's always two brothers, with what seems like different views and politics.'

I explained that my sister, Janet, is probably the healthiest member of the three children and, unlike Peter and me, she even had friends – many of them. This led the broadcaster to a rather maudlin tangent about how he doubted he had real friends, and how people in public life find true friendship very difficult to sustain. I was only making a light quip, but was now in a serious discussion about something – obviously I had triggered something that resonated deeply for him.

Whenever people ask why I may have different views

from my brother (which they have done consistently over the years), I shoot back, 'Well, do you agree with all your siblings?' Almost without exception, when I ask that I get emphatic denials, often followed by details as to why they are so different from their siblings.

The curiosity about us as brothers being seen as quite different is something that for a period attracted much attention. So much so that Hannie Rayson, one of our most well known playwrights, wrote a play called *Two Brothers* that was very loosely based on the differences between me and Peter. It is now a text on the final school year's English syllabus in Victoria. I went to see it with my family, but Peter refused. Peter was understandably upset with the portrayal of him as a heartless government minister who, in the play, gets blood on his hands through his policies. My character was the bleeding-heart leftie brother. These are the dangers of fiction mixed with a little fact.

In an ABC TV interview aired in January 2012, I was asked if things were easier now that Peter was out of politics. I said I thought he would have made a great prime minister, but power is like the ring in *The Lord of the Rings*. The one who wears it (in this case referring to John Howard) is convinced they control the ring and can give it up whenever they choose, to whomever they choose. But they soon discover the ring controls them. I went on to say that I believed John Howard should have stepped down as PM in early 2007 and passed the power, as promised, to Peter. The interviewer then asked me, 'Well, who wears the ring now?' That question threw me and I stumbled out an answer that we all wear a ring with power in our own circles and need to be conscious of our own power. As Nelson Mandela quoted in his 1994 Inaugural address, '... Our deepest fear is not that we are inadequate; our deepest fear is that we are powerful beyond measure.'

I believe that each person is entitled to make their own judgements on all things in life, be it politics, religion or their value system. I find even now as a father of three young adults that my three are all similar in some ways, yet very different in others. But I cannot as their father presume that any will be identical to me. I have no doubt I have influenced them, but I cannot control their choices and values. They are seeing things from where they sit. It reminds me of the story about the child who was sent to Sunday school with a sign pinned on his back: 'The opinions expressed by this child do not necessarily reflect those of his home.'

My brother is a committed Liberal, a strong voice for conservative values – and in this, he is very akin to my parents' political persuasions. It would be true to say we were influenced when young by the adage that 'God is in his heaven, Bob Menzies is in the Lodge, and all is well with the world'. The implication was that all true Christians voted conservative. It was somewhat of a shock for me at university to meet committed Christians who were passionate Labor supporters outraged by the dismissal of Gough Whitlam as prime minister in 1975.

I realise that I too have been influenced by where I have sat. My encounters at university were followed by a broadening political and theological education through some years of study in Europe, where I met Christians and others from a wide range of political persuasions. And then, following that, I was influenced by my years in ministry in St Kilda, where many of the local issues we came up against, such as housing shortages and the de-institutionalisation of the mentally ill, meant I was forced to look for political answers on both a local and state level. I became increasingly aligned with those looking for community answers rather than always putting the emphasis on the rights, privileges and freedoms of the individual.

But, saying that, I am not a political-party man. Too much of the maverick, I think. Or, as some have called me, a boundary rider.

Fortunately, the world is big enough for all types. And our democratic system gives people the freedom to express their views and support the candidate of their choice. The challenge for families is to accept diversity of ideas and allegiances.

So, for me, my brother's politics come as no surprise – as, in many ways, he has lived out the family script, albeit taking it much farther than my parents ever thought possible for one of their own. I think I have confused them more, as – while they have utterly supported me in my ministries and many of the stances I have taken – I know at times when the media has chosen to blow up the differences between us as brothers, it has caused them anxiety and concern. It is the price of public life and a price they have had to adjust to.

A calling to justice

I often tell the story of life as being a bit akin to climbing a ladder. The obvious ladder we climb is the one all parents inculcate in their kids. It's about what we do, what work we perform in the world.

In year twelve my mother took me aside and said, 'Tim, this is the big year. You know you are going to have to study really hard.' When I asked, 'Why?', she said, 'Because if you do study hard and do well you might get to go to university.' Back then in 1972, only about 8 per cent of us ever did.

Well, I did study reasonably hard and did well and got into a law faculty. So I had definitely climbed the first rung of the career ladder. I remember the family celebration at a Chinese restaurant. My mother took me aside and said, 'We are so proud of you, Tim. But now that you are beginning law, you realise that you are going to have to really study hard.' She explained that not everyone who got a law degree would end up doing articles with a law firm and get a job that would lead to being an attorney. I enjoyed university, and did well enough to secure articles. I had climbed another rung.

There was another family celebration, at another Chinese restaurant, and then after the congratulations my mother said, 'Of course, we are proud of you, but now that you have articles you know you must work really hard.' I asked why once again. 'Well, not everyone who gets articles is asked to stay on and given a job as a solicitor.'

When I finished and was kept on and was then admitted as a barrister and solicitor, I had climbed the next rung. So now there were about eight rungs above me and then I might be made a partner in the firm. With each rung, more pay was the reward, and more social esteem. It spelt out success and seemed to be what life was about.

But at the same time, I sensed another ladder. It is the ladder of calling, or vocation. It is more about what you are than what you do. The first rung on it is working out what gets your juices going. Your art, music, sport, volunteering, coaching or caring. You work out what you must do. If you do not do this, you are going to be poorer and the world is going to be poorer.

Vocation, according to American writer Frederick Buechner in his book *Wishful Thinking: A Theological ABC*, is 'the place where your deep gladness and the world's deep hunger meet'.

If the ladder of calling overlaps with the career ladder, you can have a fortunate union of purpose. Fancy being paid for what you are called to do! But for many people, the career ladder may pull them away from their sense of calling. The drive for success or status, or even following the family business, can mean a strong sense of disconnect with what is one's ultimate passion or longing.

For me, my calling always had to do with justice. That is why I gravitated to law, until I worked out it did not necessarily have that much to do with justice. Most lawyers are businessmen. There was an awful lot about the work that did not fulfil my need to see change brought about.

Where did this calling start? Well, perhaps it might go back to sharing a room with my brother for many years. We would have our fights and my father would storm in because we had woken him up with our squabbling. He would always say the same thing: 'I don't care who started this and who you think is to blame. I am not that interested in the story. I am going to punish you both.' That is when I got interested in justice. I reckon Peter started it more than me. Although I could be biased!

Wherever the calling started, I have always been driven by a visceral sense of righting injustice. It is the thread of calling that has led me into whatever work I have undertaken, from law to ministry, from local politics to aid and development. I know I have been fortunate to have the two ladders working together, and to be able to change direction in my working life accordingly. It is not so for all. But let me say: keep your 'deep gladness' in mind always. It is what will sustain you through the darker times, and doors may open, in ways unforeseen, for your unique contribution to be expressed.

They shall build houses and live in them

Some people have told me that my faith got hijacked by social justice. Actually, it was more that I started studying the whole story in the Old Book. From the prophets of the Hebrew Scriptures railing against injustice through to Jesus, I realised that there in that book was a picture of wellbeing or shalom for the whole world. All of life was sacred – not just the religious bits. The Hebrew Scriptures paint a picture of a society where it is not permitted to charge interest on a loan to the poor, where landowners are instructed to give the poor access to land.

Rabbi Jonathan Sachs, the Orthodox Rabbi for Great Britain, got into trouble with his community when he included too many in the love and shalom of God. His universalism went too far for his cloistered Orthodox community, who thought they knew the boundaries of Yahweh's inclusiveness. I identify as our hearts are more inclusive than are our doctrines. Bob Pierce, the founder of World Vision, wrote on the flyleaf of his Bible, 'Let my heart be broken by the things that break the heart of God'. I think the heart is a better way to know God than by propositions from the head. Rabbi Sachs taught that God is seen in the face of the poor, whoever they be. He is right.

I discovered that personal faith that transforms, and a concern for social justice, are caught up together in the wonderful Hebrew word, 'shalom'. It means peace, transformative peace. It is why I sign off all my letters with that word. Let there be shalom in your hearts, your homes, marriages and families; let there be shalom in the economy or marketplace, with shalom in your weights so that you measure the grain fairly and do not defraud the poor. Take note of that, Wall Street. Let there be shalom in your courts of justice and the way the banks lend and sell financial products to people. Let there be shalom in our politics.

In my church ministry as a pastor, and my legal work as a defence lawyer, I discovered that shalom went missing in many areas – but particularly in housing. Indeed, substandard housing and soaring rents were at the heart of many of the troubles of my St Kilda clients. I was reading the Book of Isaiah one morning, and these words hit me: 'They shall build houses and live in them. No longer shall they build houses and others live in them. They shall plant vineyards and drink from their own vines. No longer shall they plant and others drink from their vines.' This text drove me to discovering others in my local area who were passionate about housing. And that common interest took me in the direction of local politics. I stood on a platform of putting rate-payers' dollars into affordable housing for long-term poor St Kilda residents. They had lived for generations in this suburb, enjoyed the beach, public transport and access to the city some six kilometres away, and now they were being forced out. It was the first local council in Australia to prioritise the poor in this way.

At my inauguration as mayor of St Kilda, I read the words from Isaiah in my address. St Kilda has a big Jewish community who might have appreciated Isaiah, but most in the council chamber that night were secular activists who in all honesty probably cringed at the Baptist bible basher who had donned the mayoral robes and chain. But even the most secular of activists couldn't take issue with the sentiment in that quote.

Shalom in the city
of Melbourne

One of my shocks as mayor of St Kilda was the rapid introduction of slot (or poker) machines. In 1992 they were suddenly introduced, without consumer warnings to the state of Victoria. People I knew, people with homes and businesses, started to get addicted and lose everything. I was not a gambler, but neither was I a prohibitionist. But I have always worried that any joy at winning through gambling must come at the expense of someone who has lost. It is a zero-sum game, unlike the stock market where in principle it can be a win-win. With the stock market, investment spurs the creation of a bigger and better business, and speculative profits are not necessarily at the expense of someone losing.

But what infuriated me was what happened in the early 1990s in the state of Victoria: a state-sponsored gaming explosion. It was openly promoted and pushed by our elected representatives. The state unabashedly moved gambling from something that was at the margins of culture to the centre of economic wellbeing. A counterfeit shalom. In fact, our premier called for a gaming-led recovery of our economic fortunes. When spruiking and opening the biggest casino in Australia, he called it a beacon of hope and stated categorically that this casino represented the new spirit of Victoria – my state. 'Spirit' and 'hope' are powerful words.

In my legal practice I noticed a rise in people seeking help who had been law abiding, but who had become criminals. Of course, the state and the gambling industry said they were just sad people with a problem – no-one was forcing them to gamble. I knew differently. My first legal client, a woman who had stolen from her work, was called Zlata. She owned a house, had a great marriage and three beautiful children. Slots had an effect on her that seemed mystifying. Not only did she lose everything, but she was sent to prison for four years for embezzling $50,000 from her employer to chase her losses on the slots. Her character convinced me that it was not pathetic people who were to blame: these were dangerous machines that had been introduced with no consumer warnings.

I now know that they are designed to addict. In Australia, you can lose up to $10,000 in one go on one slot machine. In the UK, most machines are a one-pound load-up with maximum losses of about £40 an hour. As the latest evidence shows, Australia has the most problem gamblers in the world because we have the greatest number of the highest loss machines in the world. Between 40 and 60 per cent of the $12 billion profit from slots comes from addicted people. So much for an innocent recreation: the average loss from problem gamblers is $1200 per hour.

All of this is state sponsored and state promoted. Yet slots are the second greatest contributor to crime after illicit drugs. You don't have to play the slots to lose at them. We all lose, because our courts are clogged with crimes from the slots. Why is this allowed? Because the state is addicted to the easy gambling tax revenue from allowing more slots into the poorest suburbs. It's easier than putting up other taxes.

I have now clocked up twenty years of seeking the reform of these dangerous machines and have to remind myself that with tobacco it took over fifty years. The parallels are interesting. In both cases, if you use the product as it is designed to be used, you will become addicted. So it is not that there are just a few sad, weak and addictive personalities who are affected, meaning we should not bother our conscience or shape our policy to slow the machines down. The product itself is dangerous and designed to be addictive, particularly with the speed of Australian machines. Like the one against Big Tobacco, it will be a long battle because there is so much easy money at stake for cowardly, compromised politicians and predatory captains of the gambling industry. In both cases, there was massive capture of researchers through funding and scary advertising campaigns about a nanny state taking away the individual's rights. And there is the drip-feed of financial grants from the slots to community groups who are threatened with the tap being turned off if they speak up. The intimidation has been effective in straitened times for charities, and the silence from most charities has been deep.

The reason is simple, really. There is just so much money at stake coming from problem gamblers, so the party in government never wants to change the status quo.

So how much money do you want?

S ome years ago, my profile as a problem-gambler advocate took a rapid rise in the media. As a result, some opportunities arose from left field that gave me pause for thought. One was from a car company. Their PR and advertising firm contacted me and said they had taken the liberty of writing some scripts for me for a TV campaign for their latest model. Could they send them through? Intrigued as to what they had in mind, I gave them permission.

The script had me, full-screen, beginning with, 'Don't gamble on a used car.' Then I would go on to spruik the benefits of the latest model, finishing with a pious look down the barrel of the camera and the killer closing line: '... And that's Gospel, brother.' A big glossy advertisement.

For a two-hour shoot and a month's TV campaign, they were going to pay me $25,000. I thanked them and politely declined. A few days later, another call came through. The caller explained that his client (the car company) was very keen on using me and they would offer me $30,000. I laughed and declined again. A week later another call came. He said his client was very insistent and was prepared to pay $35,000. I firmly explained, 'Look, I am not willing to do this.'

The exasperated response was, 'Well, how much money do you want?' The penny finally dropped. In his mind, it was just a matter of price, as everyone has a price. Negotiations are not about principle, but just a matter of finding the right entry price. We would get there finally if he was persistent.

Apart from the grubbiness of undermining my stand on gambling and the trust in me as a minister to trade it all for a car sale, it illustrated a fundamental temptation and choice we can all face. In a market economy, where the natural measure of all inputs is a dollar measure, what is the price of principle? In one sense, none of us is pure and can ever escape this dilemma. But clarifying what is not for sale can help us. There are some things that no amount of money can buy.

The alleged encounter between George Bernard Shaw and a married woman is still the classic parable of our age. He offered her $10,000 to sleep with him for one night. She agonised over breaking her vows, but agreed. He said, 'Good. But I have been thinking about this. Will you sleep with me for a shilling and sixpence?'

She was outraged and said, 'That is so disgusting. What do you take me for?'

His brilliant reply was, 'We have already established that; now we are just haggling over price.'

The film *Indecent Proposal* with Demi Moore and Robert Redford is just an update on this George Bernard Shaw exchange, only this time the price tag of the proposal is $1 million for the young woman to spend one night with the older man. Interestingly, when the film came out, some married women in Melbourne were asked by a newspaper in a street vox pop whether they would break their vows and sleep with the character played by Robert Redford for $1 million. Most were recorded saying they would sleep with him for nothing!

I think the values and principles are dead easy when the offer is one shilling. We instantly recognise that this is a sleazebag wanting the woman to prostitute herself. But when it is $10,000, or $1 million as in *Indecent Proposal*, the ethical principles become cloudy and difficult. In truth, the ethical principle around loyalty and vows has not changed – only the price tag has changed. But in this culture it is slippery stuff, and we get confused.

It is tricky stuff because we have such facility to rationalise why we would do greater good with the money. It is tricky even in the church, where we are solemnly warned by Jesus that we cannot serve two masters and must choose between God and Mammon. Mammon was the Aramaic word for wealth, and Jesus surprised his hearers by suggesting Mammon was a diety. In the Greco–Roman world there were thousands of gods, but none called Mammon. What was Jesus talking about? With the rise of the Christian prosperity gospel, we see how right Jesus was to name this as the choice.

We in World Vision have seen research tracking the money flowing out of the pockets of the poor in African slums into the pockets of American prosperity evangelists through their TV programs and missions to the poor. And it is mainly one-way traffic, with far less coming back. This is depressing. They are selling a gospel of material blessing and healing with the tagline that if you give to their ministry, the Lord will bless you tenfold. This is just music to desperate ears. Now we see that Africa has its own crop of mega-rich evangelists with fleets of luxury cars and private jets, all flowing from the smooth use of a prosperity gospel.

It continues to be a source of contention in the Western church. I have had long conversations with many of my Pentecostal friends. Some honestly explain to me that the chief seduction in their world is a Love Offering. You accept a church speaking engagement on the principle that there will be a Love Offering taken up for the preacher. This is a second offering to just 'bless' the preacher because he has 'blessed' you. It is often thousands of dollars, and rarely declared for tax purposes because it is not income but a freewill gift. The big-name preachers could be seen as choosing their conference-speaking schedule after factoring in where they would clean up with Love Offerings. Those Pentecostal preachers who break with this practice on principle of transparency are criticised as ignoring God's blessing.

It is tricky stuff that goes to the heart of what the Bible says: 'love of money is the root of all evil.'

I am your new relationship manager

Merridie and I were at home having a moment of intense disagreement. I might add that this is pretty rare for us. I forget now what we were arguing about, but I do remember the phone ringing when I was in a particularly bad mood, and answering it curtly. I heard the voice of a friendly young woman say, 'Hello Mr Costello, I am Janelle from your bank and am ringing to introduce myself. I am your new relationship manager.'

I said, 'Thank you Janelle and, boy, have you rung at the right time for us. Here, I want you to speak to my wife right now and sort her out.' With that I thrust the phone into Merridie's hand. A relationship manager!

Selling me a new banking product is a bit stale. Dress it up as a relationship, and suddenly we are interested. But was Janelle interested in a relationship beyond her KPIs imposed for business banking? At least we can all work that one out. It is much more complex when you do not see it coming.

We were struggling financially in our early days at St Kilda, with a church of fifteen members who could not pay a stipend beyond a day or two a week, and a legal practice that had barely begun. Imagine our joy when a couple we had been acquainted with previously rang out of the blue and said they admired our choice to go into a hard place for ministry and wanted to help us financially. They made a time to come to lunch and explain what God had laid on their hearts to help us. We were excited and believed this to be an answer to our prayers, because the bills were mounting up and we were anxious. Lunch over and a lovely catch-up later, they again raised their conviction about helping us financially. After nice preliminaries, the punchline came. They wanted to recruit us into a pyramid scheme. They were making money. It had tremendous potential, so the spiel went. We would be an addition to their commissions and, if successful, we would make some money ourselves. This was a win-win. I cannot describe the sick feeling of disappointment in our stomachs.

A relationship from former years was their chance to turn friendship into a commercial opportunity that would just happen to also benefit them. Indeed, the idea was to use my relationships with people in the church to sell. They explained how the key was to commercialise those relationships and, as I was a great networker, they were sure that I would do well with their coaching. And churches were great natural markets – where else do such reliable solid citizens, who pay their bills and do not renege on their contracts, meet each week? We politely declined. But we did feel angry.

Family, friendship and trust are essential parts of social capital, and it is legitimate to understand them as a foundation for prosperity. The Harvard sociologist Robert Putnam has a delightful study of two provinces in Italy with similar demography and economic opportunities. One was prospering and the other struggling. Why, when they enjoyed similar comparative advantages? Putnam's main conclusion was that the success of the region that was thriving was mainly due to the widespread existence of choral societies. Yes: choirs were the key to economic growth. When people came together to sing, they went out for coffee and pizza after and talked about their kids, community and businesses. Out of conversation, trust was built for new partnerships and trade. A shared friendship led to creativity and innovation. It was why one of my first acts when I became CEO of World Vision Australia was to encourage the creation of a staff choir. Though I struggle to carry a tune myself, the WVA Freedom Choir is going strong after eight years, regularly performing at staff functions and community festivals.

All cultures have to find the fine line between unconditional friendship and social-capital sparking economic self-interest and advancement. If we fail to receive unreciprocated acts of friendship free of any taint of self-interest, we become cynical and suspicious. That is the definition of friendship. But if there is transparency and no manipulation, let friendships be the springboard to commercial opportunities. But knowing that we are not being used under the cover of friendship is pretty fundamental, even for relationship managers!

As a postscript, Merridie tells me our manager was invaluable a few years later when we sold our home and bought another. The personal trust by then had been established. I guess some things can change with time, when genuine needs arise.

Civility in all relationships

I almost always travel economy when I fly, domestically or internationally. In fact, no matter how long I am away for I always carry only hand luggage in order to make quick exits. I manage this by carrying a few drip-dry shirts that I wash under the shower at night and wring out and hang up to dry.

One time, I had been up in Sumatra responding to an earthquake, without much sleep for seventy-two hours. I was pleased to be heading home.

First stop was Bali, and then Melbourne. As I came through the exit at Bali with our World Vision Indonesia director Trihardi, a crowd was waiting that included a middle-aged Australian I had never met. He recognised me and made some wrong assumptions, since I was coming out first. From where he stood, he launched into a loud tirade of personal abuse – loud enough for most bystanders to hear. Pointing at me he said, 'That is exactly why I have stopped giving to charity – because you fly at the pointy end of the plane and waste my money.' I politely took him on, telling him I only fly economy, as do all our staff, and I was coming out first because I only had hand luggage.

At that point, rather than step back or apologise, he continued, shouting, 'Well, other charities have CEOs who fly business class, and you are all the same and none of you is going to get another cent from me.' I thanked him for his support in the past and walked on.

My Indonesian colleague looked at me in shock and utter amazement and asked me if all Australians were like that. Did I cop this a lot? It got me thinking about civility. Are we losing it?

I have always believed that even if you are angry and it is justified, treating another person with respect is non-negotiable. Words are spears, and attacking the person, not the idea, is taking root as the new norm. Many point to a drop in standards. Take schoolchildren to our national parliament's question time and they cannot believe the abuse and behaviour. They are told never to behave like that and yet there are their nation's leaders, who they see on the news every night, acting in a way that would earn them a rebuke and a detention.

I have been a long-time admirer of Vaclav Havel, the former president of Czechoslovakia who recently died. I read his plays in the early 1980s, when he was locked up by the communist leaders for his truth-telling. I visited the old Czechoslovakia in 1983 while it was still under the communists, and I was able to meet with some Charter 77 dissidents. Havel had been the founder of this charter and its human rights initiatives, and had paid for them with the loss of his freedom. The man only grew in stature in my eyes as I watched him later on TV and saw him in the role of the president of

Czechoslovakia. He was always bowing to people – great or small – and showing the utmost courtesy. Yes, he was a quaint European gentleman, but one whose civility to all included the former enemies who had hounded him to prison and ill health. If he and Nelson Mandela can retain clear convictions and still show such courtesy to the people who wanted them dead, and with whom they violently disagree, why cannot our leaders do the same? Particularly when our leaders have barely a cigarette paper's width of ideological difference between them? Is it that hard to model civility?

I was addressing civility in a breakfast speech to the nation's politicians in parliament. I told them the story of Stanley Milgram's famous experiment at Yale. He advertised for people to volunteer for a scientific experiment into pain thresholds. Good people signed up and were told that they were to stand in front of a machine and, under instructions, turn knobs that increased the voltage. Through glass they could see an actor (though they were not told he was acting) connected to wires and receiving shocks through the wires. He writhed and screamed as they turned up the voltage. The actor requested they stop, explaining he had a heart condition. Despite this warning, because the experimenters urged them to continue, these good people turned the knobs and watched his torment. Milgram was thrown out of Yale for such an unethical experiment. But he had justified the defence of Nazis who were on trial after the Second World War: they claimed that they could not be judged, as anyone would have done what they did under orders. He had shown that context – in this case scientific – influenced ethics and behaviour much more than character. These were good people who complied and, by so doing, did something bad.

I said to some of our nation's leaders, 'I know you are good people and you went into politics to make a difference. In normal life, you do not shout others down, or take such glee when they stumble or are embarrassed. You do not point at and abuse others – so what is it about the context of parliamentary question time, where the nation sees you behave like this?

An earnest backbencher came up to me. It was the first time I had met Kevin Rudd. He said that what I said was challenging, and he wanted to write a book on better ethics and behaviour for politicians. Would I help? I smiled and replied that it had been written already. He asked for the title and I said, '*Rules of the House.* You already have the book and that is not the problem – what becomes a problem is the context.'

Civility has to be cultivated; it is a learned art. Australians can do a lot better at it in all contexts – be it Bali airports or parliament, sporting fields or even supermarket car parks!

Is there life tonight?

My generation was different from my parents', and my children's is different from mine. But is it substance or just style?

My parents' generation appeared to focus on one question: is there life after death? I understand this, when they lived through the Great Depression and the Second World War, shaped by parents who themselves lived through the war to end all wars. We forget that, until the US entered the Second World War, Hitler and fascism were ascendant across Europe and the rest of Europe was communist. Great Britain was on her knees and the Japanese, even before obliterating Pearl Harbor, had taken British Malaya and were headed to Singapore (which they took). Australia, it was assumed, was next in line. The light we call democracy was flickering out. This was a generation that knew how fragile all we take as so solid could be. It could not be taken for granted. Life was tough economically, and the view that this was a vale of tears and a testing ground for the next world made sense. So many young lives were lost. Every street had its grief to share. So faith and character were needed to pass the test. This meant saving, not spending.

My father was forced to leave school at fourteen and go to work in a factory because of the Depression. He married late (at thirty-four) because it was considered irresponsible to propose to a woman before you had saved a full house deposit and shown you could properly provide. It meant digging deep in times of personal pain to find resources within oneself, not opting for easy instant solutions. Therapy was unheard of, and he learnt to stoically suffer rather than complain. When we were young, my father chose not to tell us any stories about the deprivations and terrors of war, where he fought the Japanese in Papua New Guinea and nearly died of malaria on the boat home. The worst thing was a whinger or a crybaby. Tears might be shed, but in private. As Adam Lindsay Gordon put it:

> *Life is mostly froth and bubble,*
> *Two things stand like stone:*
> *Kindness in another's trouble.*
> *Courage in your own.'*
> (Finis Exoptatus)

So hope was telescoped to the next world. Many of the hymns my parents loved were about crossing over to a land that was whiter than snow. That land was certainly not the Struggle-town experienced down here. I would wonder as a child at how much their eyes would shine as they sang loudly in church of that future place. Hope was caught up with answering the big question, 'Is there life beyond death?' Reading the obituary columns in the paper was a civic duty, and attending the funerals a solemn act of love even though feelings were expressed in mute voices.

My generation watched their stoicism and was puzzled. Our question was not theirs. Ours was, 'Is there life before death?' Things seemed to be so staid and their conservative taboos were life-constricting and irrational. Why not live to the full now? Why postpone pleasure and hope? With the 1960s, when I grew up, the shackles of any moral constraints were thrown off. We might have seen the Depression mentality of saving, not spending, in our parents, but we had something denied them in their youth – credit. This meant we could have it right now and worry about paying it off later. In fact, we became the highest spending, worst saving generation in history. The Australian government had to introduce compulsory superannuation to force us to save – a brilliant policy choice. My parents made their first trip to Europe in their late fifties. Merridie and I were off to live there by the age of twenty-five.

But in our defence, our focus on living now did raise some good questions about why some were missing out now. How come it was all men running government, business and the Church? Where were the women? Thus the rise of feminism, arguing for the inclusion of obvious leadership options for half our population. In any event, it was ridiculous. We knew that it was not the men but their wives who really ran the Church and propped up the men to maintain the fiction of male leadership.

We asked, 'How come Aboriginal people have been left out of Australian history in a conspiracy of silence?' And soon a rights movement developed, uniting Aboriginals and young people, that allowed them to be full citizens and enjoy the possibility of a full life before death. And we asked, 'Where do we see migrants in positions of power? Is there prejudice against those for whom English is a second language?' So we saw the birth of multiculturalism. The parallels with the civil rights movement and the anti-colonial and pro-peace movements elsewhere may have been driven by a concern for life before death.

The next generation never ceases to surprise me. As I watch them through my blinkers and fret that they do not have the moral seriousness of my generation, I see a different question at play. Not 'is there life after death' or 'is there life before death', but 'is there life tonight?' Is there a party or action happening now? It has all sped up, and I am feeling slow and old. Ever wasted time as a parent sending out an invitation for a twenty-first birthday with an RSVP date? This generation hangs loose and rarely RSVPs, because then you are committed and somewhat stuck if a better option comes along. You need to be free to maximise the moment. If nothing better comes along, cruise in to the twenty-first and pity help the poor caterer. Marriage is postponed because that is a big set of weights when flexibility and mobility are critical in a fast-changing world. But I have learned that the idealism is still there, and they will make a difference – just in their own way.

The difference is style rather than substance. Maybe this is a penetrating insight into the obvious, but I think no generation is better or worse – just different, because the context is different. Each generation has its wisdom and life experience to pass on, and each has its shadow side.

Kids rarely do what their parents tell them, but curiously they often end up doing what their parents do. My son Elliot set up a charity called Y-GAP with a couple of friends in 2009. It stands for Y Generation Against Poverty. They do project work in Africa and Asia for education and against trafficking. I find it fascinating that they raise much of their income for Y-GAP from parties. What I see is that you have to cut the wood with the grain, and if the generation likes to party, then … ? To party for poverty still rankles with me, but then what were Live Aid and other benefit concerts? Is it wrong to have fun and slip in a serious purpose, if that is the lifestyle option?

They are also serious about social enterprise and how business models intersect with social outcomes. Elliot helped start, under the banner of Y-GAP, a commercial coffee shop in Melbourne's CBD called Kinfolk, where after your purchase you deposit a coffee bean in one of three jars. The beans are then counted and all the profits go proportionately to the respective three charities – one of which is a Y-GAP project in Africa. Y-GAP is serious about exploring social business. This is where as an investor you are promised no loss, but also no financial dividend. Instead, you take some equity, but only receive a social dividend, such as helping to eradicate trafficking or domestic homelessness.

I should have picked this direction in Elliot. I remember his business skills and fascination with making money at an early age. Our pocket money was patchy, so he took matters into his own hands at the age of six. Unbeknown to us, he drew some stick-figure drawings and put prices like a dollar or 50 cents on each, and set up a stall at the front gate. He made $13 from people passing by on a Saturday morning. When he came inside clutching the money, I falsely accused him of stealing it. With tears in his eyes, he said he had made it and took me to his street table.

At twelve, he had a local paper round and cleverly subcontracted a few of his extra jobs out to his friends for a commission. I remember us having a cash-flow problem at one time and having to borrow from him, as at that point he had more money in the bank than us. We lay awake in bed that night, worried that he was going to charge interest!

He didn't. Perhaps this was the birth of his social conscience and social business instincts.

Eat, drink and be merry

One of our sons' friends, a co-worker in their charity Y-GAP, dropped in to get some advice. I had not seen him for a while and commented on how great he looked. He said he had given up drinking and had not touched a drop in eight months. I asked why.

He replied that after travelling to developing countries and feeling so alive, despite the poverty, with the simple celebration of family and community, he had come back to Australia and fallen back into a lifestyle of well-lubricated partying and socialising. He started to feel bad and wondered why he had such joy with people who had nothing – but could sing and dance, without alcohol – and why he felt bad here. He noticed that his youth culture was alcohol-saturated and that friendship was unthinkable without a drink. It intensified his personal problems, and so he gave it up completely.

This was not all that easy, as his refusal to drink raised suspicions and fears that he was different or judging. He wasn't – but a culture is by definition averse to those who do not follow its norms. On Australia Day, he said he was with friends in St Kilda and, by the end of the day, he was the only one sober. The deterioration in all those around him was distressing to watch. It was an eye-opener to realise that once was him. Worse, it is nationally demanded to have a drink to be considered patriotic.

Was this a religious conversion that changed him? No. Had he joined a cult? No. He had just noticed how dependent his generation had become on defining a party or a good time as a drinking session, and opted out.

I did not drink until I was twenty-six. My father has been a teetotaller all his life. He is still alive at ninety-three, which says something for abstinence. My mother said she was a teetotaller after she married my father, and that she only kept the brandy in the cupboard for use in the Christmas plum puddings she made. But it seemed to evaporate well before the Christmas cooking started! In Europe, where Merridie and I studied, we starting imbibing. It was cultural and, even in a Baptist seminary in Switzerland, most students drank. It's hard to have a meal without wine when you live in Europe for four years. Especially when you regularly share meals with Italians.

But as I listened to my son's friend, I felt a sense of solidarity. He is right. It is hard to not conform in this culture. As a Baptist, I come from a dissenting tradition. John Bunyan, the famous Baptist preacher, was in Bedford Prison for religious dissent when he wrote the classic, *The Pilgrim's Progress*. It is a non-conformist tradition that eschews the sensual pleasures of Bunyan's 'Mr Worldly Wiseman'.

The basic truth I realised in that moment of clarity sparked by this young man was simpler. We can all be seduced by the culture around us. It takes courage not to conform. But, surprisingly, it feels much better when we don't.

The voice of a survivor

I was in a taxi in Rwanda, being driven to Hotel Rwanda. The taxi driver had an awful scar across his whole face. I politely enquired how it had happened. He said that in the genocide of 1994 he was being chased by the murderous Hutu militias, so he fled to his church to be saved and protected. Instead, the minister let the militias know he was there and called them in to murder all the huddled people seeking safety – mostly women and children.

He was slashed with a machete and feigned death among the bodies. I will never forget his chilling words. 'I attended this church and had been saved there, but it was they who handed me over to be murdered.' Rwanda, the most Christian of African nations, was a failure of the Gospel to rise above tribalism and genocide.

As a result of a Y-GAP trip to Africa in 2009 with twenty other young people, my son met a young man named David Mwambari in Uganda. A firm friendship grew, and Elliot encouraged David to consider moving to Melbourne when he was seeking to undertake further studies into the effects of the genocide on young people. As a result of that meeting, David lived in our home in

Melbourne for a month while he got organised to do a doctorate through one of our finest universities.

David is a Rwandan. He is now thirty-one. His story is one none of us could imagine living through.

At the time of the Rwandan genocide, in April 1994, David's family, who were both Hutu and Tutsi, were at their home in Butare, which is in the south of Rwanda. Butare was still a safe haven for Tutsis and other mixed ethnic people at that point. The mayor of Butare had refused to permit anyone to carry out the genocide. But within a few days of making that decree, the mayor was killed – and anyone who did not agree with the propaganda to exterminate the Tutsis was equally persecuted.

At the house where David was hiding with his family were Tutsis, Hutus and mixed families who gathered to pray every day after they had heard of the massacres in other areas of Rwanda. Groups of hungry young people would often show up at their door between the sprees they undertook at the command of some self-appointed leader. Some would carry machetes and have blood on their hands and faces. The family would feed them as best they could with what food they had. Once, they were saved from a youthful mob by the presence and pleas of the grandmother of one of the leaders – she happened to be at David's house praying.

Without any telephones or any other communication facilities, they did not know who to call. They waited for death, praying. There were breaks when the killers rested for a day or two, and people went to the market, but the madness always resumed. The family was constantly threatened that they would be killed soon.

After a few months of waiting and hiding, the family was given a final warning and a death appointment. David's father (who was a recently ordained Anglican pastor) found a phone and called the Anglican bishop in his native hometown, which was in another province, to inform him that the next day they were to be killed. He was phoning to say goodbye.

The bishop did not hesitate to act and sent a driver and another pastor with an official letter saying that David's father was being transferred to work as a pastor in another diocese. It took the family two days to go through roadblocks on a journey that would now only take about one hour by car. They negotiated using the letter, and a few times were stopped and forced out of the car. They stood by the road, waiting to be killed. At one roadblock, the wait was five hours. As they waited at one of these stops someone who knew the family passed by and, at high risk to their own life, pleaded for their safety.

They later heard that the house in Butare was ambushed on the afternoon they left, the killers angry that the family had escaped. Everyone remaining there was immediately slaughtered. After David's family arrived at their destination, the same bishop then helped them all escape together from Rwanda and to settle in Kenya.

Back in Rwanda, David's family lost their grandfather, uncles and some other relatives. His grandfather was a leader of his village who had built a church and a school to educate his community.

David has dedicated himself to the future of his country and to fulfilling his grandfather's dream in Ntenyo, Rwanda. He set up a charity called Sanejo and, through a partnership with Y-GAP, David and his friends from different countries, including my own son and teams from Australia, have rebuilt much of the ruined school and added classrooms and facilities. The school is now winning prizes as a centre of excellence in educating the next generation.

A phoenix is rising from the ashes.

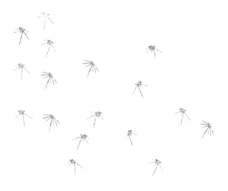

The yellow brick road

I still feel emotional when I hear recordings of Dorothy (played by Judy Garland) singing 'Somewhere over the Rainbow'. What child has not been inspired by this epic journey, in which a straw man realises he has a heart, a cowardly lion finally finds courage and a tin man discovers his brain?

Thanks to MGM's movie, the story is embedded in our culture. All of us can remember being enthralled by that story as children, and being taken back to that place as adults, surrounded by our own children's wide-eyed wonder as they too watched it. For Dorothy it was all just a dream. Well, that's how MGM chose to picture it. But it was not so originally. L. Frank Baum, the author of *The Wonderful Wizard of Oz* in 1900, saw it otherwise. In his mind, this is a story of a real journey and the real whirlwinds of life that pick us up and throw us into an entirely new place. He believed that there was a parallel universe – a spiritual world – and that our journey here has a spiritual dimension. I agree.

This story is called the original American fairytale because it illustrated how a new nation could truly develop and be great if its people would discover that the courage and heart and mind that seem so absent in daily and public life are within reach. Fairytale, yes, but deadly serious in the point it was exploring.

Real life is full of dangers, and more often than not we do not respond with heart or courage or a good mind, given the challenges we face. It takes a journey into the ambiguities of our own failures and fears to face this truth. It takes being stripped of all the safe comforts we build around ourselves to protect ourselves from vulnerability. The journey we are all on is to recognise what we are missing is actually here with us.

Kerry Packer and near death

S ome months before he died, I met up with Kerry Packer, Australia's richest man at that time. I was there to thank him for the support he had given, through Channel 9 and the international cricket match that had been held in Melbourne in January 2005, to raise money for the Asian tsunami disaster. We had a long conversation in his office in Sydney, just the two of us. His feet were up on his desk as he puffed on a few cigarettes. Clearly, he was up for a long chat. His office had retro 1950s paintings of African wildlife, although I don't think he was deliberately intending to be retro. The chat was free-ranging and mainly about ethics.

He complimented me that I stood up for ethics as, in his mind, we were losing them in our nation. When he asked where my ethics came from, I talked about my faith as the substratum. He agreed and said that, although he was not religious at all, the Sunday school and bible classes he'd had to attend as a boarder at the exclusive church school Geelong Grammar had been useful. He confessed that he had hated Sundays in the Anglican boarding school, as you could not watch TV, do sport or have fun – but, despite that, some of that religion had taught him ethics. For that he was grateful.

We got onto hope and there being life beyond death. That launched him. 'Son,' he said, 'I have been there, and take it from me – there is nothing there.' He repeated his now-famous story about when he was pronounced clinically dead from a heart attack, only to be brought back because, fortuitously enough, an ambulance happened to be passing. Having been declared dead, he spoke with the gravitas of someone who knew. 'Son, there was nothing. No light, no voice, no consciousness – nothing. This is the only life we have. When it is over, it is over.'

At one level, I agree with the bluntness that challenges shallow faith. There are many versions of Christian faith that do not take this life seriously enough because of an escape-ladder belief that the next one is the real one. At its crudest, it translates into not worrying about changing anything down here, because it is all going to pass away. I personally do not subscribe to that view of this life at all. For this reason, I respected Kerry Packer's honesty that said to live now and refuse any deathbed conversions of convenience. It reminded me of what Voltaire reputedly said on his deathbed after being exhorted by the priest to renounce the devil and all his works: 'This is no time to be making new enemies!'

Of course, experience is notoriously subjective. Very recently I bumped into Ian, a surgeon and one of my old school buddies who I had not seen for over twenty years.

We were both waiting with our wives to see a play. We did the usual scanning of the landscape for news from acquaintances from the last twenty years. Then his wife broke in with another level of seriousness. 'Why do men have the ability to always miss the big stuff?'

She went on to tell me that he was a miracle. Ten weeks before, he had left his job at the hospital for the day and, as he drove out of the car park, he had what seems to have been a major heart attack at the tender age of fifty-six. He was only saved because it happened in a hospital car park, and they rushed him into emergency. My friend took over the conversation and told me that, unlike Kerry Packer, he had this experience of tremendous light. He remembered thinking, This is wonderful – and it was not at all scary. Indeed, it felt wonderful. The next thing he knew, he was waking up in a hospital bed connected to tubes.

He is not religious. He was not saying this to me because I am. It was just a bald statement of fact from one who is very scientific and grounded. So who is right – my school friend or Kerry? If only Kerry could tell us, now his journey has been taken in full.

For heaven's sake!

One of my friends is Andrew Knight, the Melbourne-based writer of the TV series *Seachange* and many other great film and TV scripts. I had him, along with the actor Sigrid Thornton, come in to speak at our staff gathering one year. As friends of World Vision, it was great to engage in their thoughts. Andrew told staff he was a supporter of World Vision, but never got the Christian bit. When I asked what bit in particular, he said, 'Heaven.' For him, the thought of an eternity of floating on a cloud, playing the harp and doing daily Bible classes was not a sufficient appeal to hope. He added, somewhat tongue-in-cheek, 'You really need to do better than that – at least the Muslims seem to offer virgins in the afterlife.'

I think he is spot-on. And very funny. Though many Christians prescribe to this version of heaven, you will not find it in the Bible. The picture of heaven is God's rule on earth. As pictured in the last book of the New Testament, the New Jerusalem has no need for walls (as there are no enemies or war) – it is a human community on earth, with all peoples of every tongue and tribe streaming into it.

It parallels the Lord's Prayer, which most of us can still stumble through from childhood memory. 'Your will be done on earth, as it is in heaven. Your Kingdom come,' here and now! Heaven was never about the sky and ethereal clouds. It was about justice and the end of suffering and tears here on earth.

That changes my view of what should be done now. The struggle for justice and the bruises and marks of suffering here and now are honoured. Just as in the resurrected Christ, the spear wounds and nail prints were still in his body; they could be touched. They were not obliterated by resurrection, as an escape from this world and its history. Christian hope has continuity between what happens here and the future.

Sitting with death

Merridie's eldest brother, Dr Paul Kitchen, died less than twelve weeks after having a brain tumour diagnosed in October 2011. He was a magnificent surgeon who had dedicated much of his life to advancing the treatment of breast cancer surgery in Melbourne, as well as serving in a hospital in Nazareth, Israel. The latter was voluntary work, which he undertook every couple of years for a few weeks at a time. He would be accompanied by groups of Australians who would do practical work around the hospital and some nearby schools. Paul and his wife, Merrill, had worked there in the mid-1970s for a few years and had fallen in love with the land, its people and history.

Because Paul declined so rapidly, around Christmas we cancelled our planned summer holidays. In fact, he passed away early on the 27th of December. It meant we all had time to be together as a family. It was an insight into how it takes time to grieve properly. I have done many funerals in my time, and have often felt that in our culture we do not take enough time for death. The funerals can be pretty rushed; people pay their respects and get back to work. The funeral for

Paul lasted two hours on a hot January afternoon, with thirteen people giving tributes, none of which repeated anything about his life; there was so much to share. It was a brilliant testimony to a brilliant life. Nobody wanted the service to conclude. You really felt justice had been done to a wonderful man who had been cut down so cruelly.

The next morning saw another service, with just the family in attendance at the crematorium. Everyone was able to say some heartfelt words as we gathered around his coffin. We were privileged to share a number of family times with his wife, children and grandchildren. To sit with a family going through the cycles of grief is important. But it takes time. No wonder our Indigenous peoples call it 'Sorry time', where all other things cease to matter for as long as is needed until the person has been honoured and the people of the community can resume their lives.

In the season of mourning that has followed, of course our thoughts have travelled to what our hopes are for life after death. It is not the time for glib answers.

My conviction is that there is a spiritual realm of which we know only the smallest amount at this stage. I know many would argue that death is death – and that all we have is the memory to hold on to.

Something deep in me resonates with a deeper hope. I have no problem in accepting the Scriptural verse, 'Oh death, where is thy victory?' I believe ultimately death has been defeated. There is a resurrection of the whole person as vindicated by the resurrection of Jesus Christ. Another verse in Scripture says we only see things dimly now, but then it will be revealed in full measure. But the full measure will include a renewed earth, where there will be justice for all.

Them geraniums

The funeral that left the deepest impression on me was my grandmother's. She died when was I only twenty-four, and I was asked to speak at it. It was a large funeral. Her minister shocked us by opening the funeral with the words: 'You can't kill Jessie Northrop! No-one can kill Jessie Northrop.' We all sat there thinking, You're right. She was indomitable.

Jessie grew up on the rural outskirts of Melbourne and trained to be a nurse. Aside from the nursing training, she was largely a self-educated woman, and she had the most amazing memory. She could recite poetry for hours. She loved reading and would write letters to all sorts of people. She was politically active and became a foundation member of the Liberal Party. As kids, we loved staying with her and soaking up the wisdom and playfulness.

I remember one weekend cooking all day with her and wondering who needed that much food. The next day she went to church and, after Sunday lunch, packed the food into baskets. With me in tow carrying one of them, she took the baskets to neighbours and to the sick and lonely people in the area. Many were people she had barely met. She had simply heard they were struggling or 'poorly'. I asked her why we were doing this, and I remember the curt reply: 'Because this is what you do.' It was so obviously an expression of her faith. What simplicity.

Living on her own at the age of eighty-two, with her husband in hospital care, she had a stroke. She was in a coma for about a week, and never came out of it. The only words she spoke were addressed to my aunt: 'Don't forget to water them geraniums.' This puzzled us all, as she did not have any geraniums in her garden. It wasn't even the way she would usually speak. We assumed it was some random disconnected thought.

It was not until after the funeral that we discovered a Henry Lawson story called 'Water them Geraniums'. If she had read it to us, no-one could remember. Told through the eyes of a rich neighbour, the story is of a woman who battles to raise a tribe of kids on her own. She is dirt poor. But her pride and joy in her impoverished world are her colourful pots of geraniums. Like so many melancholy Lawson stories, it ends on a tragic note. She is dying. As a reader, you imagine her panic. Who will feed and clothe these kids when she is gone? What will happen to them?

The last scene is where her children gather around her bed. Her last words to them are, 'Now don't forget to water them geraniums.' Whatever Grandma intended, I sensed her speaking to us from the grave. It does not matter what fame you have or money you make. What matters is whether you have done the little things – the unseen, everyday, pedestrian things. That is the measure of who you are and what your faith and life are worth.

Just keep on watering them geraniums.